Assessment to Promote Deep Learning

Linda Suskie, editor

Major Addresses From
"Rising Expectations for Assessment: Can We Deliver?"
AAHE Assessment Conference 2000
June 14-18, Charlotte, North Carolina

Jorge Klor de Alva
Noel Entwistle
James Anderson
Victor Borden
Jean MacGregor, Vincent Tinto, and Jerri Holland Lindblad
Barbara Wright

Highlights of Plenary Addresses From
"Assessment as Evidence of Learning:
Serving Student and Society"
AAHE Assessment Conference 1999
June 13-16, Denver, Colorado

Thomas A. Angelo, Peter T. Ewell, and Cecilia López
John Biggs
Sharon Robinson

ASSESSMENT TO PROMOTE DEEP LEARNING:
Insight from AAHE's 2000 and 1999 Assessment Conferences
Edited by Linda Suskie

Stylus Publishing, LLC
22883 Quicksilver Drive
Sterling, VA 20166-2102
Tel.: 1-800-232-0223 / Fax: 703-661-1547
www.Styluspub.com

ISBN 1-56377-048-2

Contents

Foreword

by Linda Suskie

Nothing is more exciting than when a student "gets it" — hones a new skill, makes an important connection, achieves deepened understanding, develops a true love of the subject. It's the reward for everything we do. But finding out, with confidence and clarity, exactly what our students have learned is a tremendous challenge, and that's where assessment comes in.

The excitement of our adventure is that we don't have all the answers yet! Higher education today faces many rising expectations: for student learning, institutional effectiveness, accountability, integrating classroom and out-of-class experiences, using instructional technology effectively, and delivering programs of outstanding quality and public credibility in a time of constrained resources. *Rising Expectations for Assessment: Can We Deliver?*, the theme of AAHE's 2000 Assessment Conference, captures the spirit of our quest for the best ways to meet rising expectations for higher education by assessing fairly and honestly and using our findings to improve what we do.

The major speakers at the 2000 Conference have laid the groundwork for our quest by giving us a strong understanding of what we already know and the challenges that lie before us. None does this more effectively than Jorge Klor de Alva, now president and chief executive officer of the parent company of the University of Phoenix, a large and successful for-profit institution. In a plenary session conversation with Gail Mellow, he explains how the University of Phoenix defines and assesses its learning outcomes and uses that information to develop its programs. While some of those in traditional higher education settings have concerns about the University of Phoenix's approach, this new model will remain a viable force, so it's important, at the very least, to understand it, and perhaps to consider adapting some aspects of its approach to assessment.

Comedian Don Novello once did a bit about the "Five Minute University." His premise was that we don't remember more than about five minutes' worth of knowledge from our college education, so why not go to college for just five minutes? We want far more than that, of course; we want to promote the deep, insightful learning that endures, and that's why Noel Entwistle's plenary remarks are vital to us all. He builds on the findings of years of research to give us valuable suggestions for ways to create curricula, pedagogies, and assessments that promote deep learning.

It's becoming increasingly clear

that treating students equitably does *not* mean treating them all the same, because students have varying backgrounds and temperaments that affect how they learn. James Anderson, keynote speaker for the conference's "Rising Expectations for Teaching and Learning" theme track, discusses cultural differences in learning styles and suggests ways to adapt our teaching and assessment strategies to meet the needs of diverse learners.

One of the latest buzzwords for demonstrating institutional effectiveness is "performance indicators." Victor Borden, keynote speaker for the "Rising Expectations for Institutional Effectiveness" track, draws on a book he coedited on performance indicators to share the characteristics of effective performance indicators and how to choose the best performance indicators for your particular situation.

One of the exciting pedagogical developments of the last few years has been the growth of the learning communities movement. Jean MacGregor, Vincent Tinto, and Jerri Holland Lindblad, keynote speakers for the "Rising Expectations for Program Quality" track, share lessons learned from assessments of learning communities. From those lessons, they reveal the secrets to assessing any innovative program successfully.

The accreditation and assessment movements have had a collaborative relationship for many years. Barbara Wright, keynote speaker for the "Rising Expectations for Excellence in Assessment Practices" track, reviews that history and offers suggestions on how we can use both assessment and accreditation to promote cultural change.

As the late-night commercials say, ". . . but that's not all!" This volume also includes highlights of *Assessment as Evidence of Learning: Serving Student and Society*, AAHE's 1999 Assessment Conference.

Tom Angelo, Peter Ewell, and Cecilia López discuss three major forces having impacts on the assessment movement — accountability demands, growing diversification in postsecondary education, and the new teaching/learning paradigm — and they remind us of the lessons we've already learned. John Biggs echoes Noel Entwistle's ideas on how our assessments influence how students study and learn and how we can promote "deep" learning. And Sharon Robinson analyzes several definitions of a "fair" test and offers suggestions on ways we can help all students demonstrate their understanding effectively.

As we continue our quest for the best possible assessment models and tools, these talented, knowledgeable individuals have laid a strong, thought-provoking foundation on which we can build.

■

Director of AAHE's Assessment Forum at the time of its 2000 Assessment Conference, **Linda Suskie** *is director of planning, assessment, and analysis at Millersville University of Pennsylvania.*

A Conversation With Jorge Klor de Alva

interviewed by Gail Mellow

*I*n an article in Educause, *Barry Munitz, former chancellor of the California State University system, talked about the way the family farm was changed by the introduction of the intercontinental railroad. Because of the change in delivery system, every form and function of the family farm changed.*

It's a very apt analogy for what the University of Phoenix may be doing for higher education. The University blasted onto the radar screen of higher education about four or five years ago (even though it's been around much longer) with a national curriculum in a for-profit setting, multiple sites, and a predominantly part-time faculty of practitioners. This very large and successful institution's model has challenged many of our long-standing ideas about the form and function of higher education.

Let's begin, Jorge, with an overview of your vision for the University of Phoenix as an innovative campus in delivering higher education.

Before I say a few things about the University and its innovations, I want to qualify my statements with the fol-

lowing: It's important to understand that our mission is to focus on students who are at least 23 years old and who are employed. We deal exclusively with employed adults — working professionals — a sector of the student spectrum that is geared for the kind of education we provide. I don't want to suggest that everything we do can be replicated in any setting.

Given that proviso, what do we do and how do we do it? Since its beginning, the University has focused on doing research on what adults (students 23 years old and older) need to be able to get into higher education and complete their studies. Through much trial and error, we developed a particular formula, which can be summarized as follows.

First, our students want to be able to go to school while working full time. So our courses are taught year-round in a highly concentrated format, each course being either five or six weeks long. We can make our courses very concentrated because our students take only one course at a time.

Second, discipline is critical if adults are to complete their education.

We know we must give our students an excuse to put millions of other far more important things aside so that they can get on with the business of their education. They need the excuse to be able to buckle down, and we had to assist them in developing it. So we set up a system of mandatory attendance. If you miss more than one class of a course at the University of Phoenix, no matter what the excuse, you are administratively dropped. If you're an online student and you do not log on five out of seven days for meaningful work, no matter what the excuse, you're administratively dropped. Raising the bar to failure with discipline is the "secret sauce" in our recipe, and that can be applied to many other settings.

Third, our more than 7,100 faculty members, of whom some 240 are full-time, are overwhelmingly practitioners. They must be trained how to teach and, since they don't have tenure, we've had to replace all the systems that are the positive sides of having tenure. We have replaced those systems through comprehensive, continuous, and rigorous processes of assessment, beginning with the identification of potential faculty, during their training, and all through their career. They are not only continually assessed but also given the tools to overcome whatever weaknesses they may have.

The underlying assumption of the University of Phoenix model is that if you can't measure something, you cannot manage it. In order to grow into a national university, we have had to know how to continually improve both academic and administrative processes. We therefore believe that everything must be assessed on a regular basis. In short, we measure — as we say

— everything that moves, regularly and thoroughly.

Let's return to your target audience and your delivery mechanism for meeting their needs. Tell us more about how you did the assessment that allowed you to determine how to package the education you present to students. How did you learn how to package what I'd call the University of Phoenix "brand," a distinctive way of offering education?

Before we do anything, we undertake studies. We tend to do relatively extensive, and frequently very expensive, studies before we enter a market, produce a new program, or make significant changes within the institution. We continually conduct focus groups throughout the country to understand the issues we should be addressing. We repeatedly survey not only our students but also their employers. Before anything gets out the door, a lot of investment has gone into figuring out what the real and perceived needs are — what we are really trying to address and the impact our moves will have.

Let me give you an example. Before we enter a market, we have a list of some 400 issues that must be researched. That includes everything that we can understand, not only about the demographic and economic setting but also about the technology infrastructure, the number and types of degrees that people have, and the programs already available in the region. We undertake a long, detailed analysis of all this information before we make a judgment about how we should respond to a particular market or curricular opportunity.

Because we continually assess and

survey our students, all of whom are employed, and our faculty, most of whom are employed elsewhere, we're continually gaining information about what employers need and therefore what employees need. That forms a big part of the beginning of any analysis of what programs we should develop.

This is a very different model from traditional higher education. (I taught for twenty-seven years in traditional institutions, so I am familiar with their secret sauces!) At traditional institutions, new programs often begin with very creative faculty members who develop them on their own and then take great pride in getting them through an understandably hesitant bureaucracy.

At the University of Phoenix, new programs usually begin with faculty members who are "out there" and who tell us, "In our company we're facing these kinds of problems. Is this true in companies all over the country?" Well, we go out and try to find out. And if it's true that these problems are happening all over and they're not being addressed, the idea is put into the hopper, so to speak, to begin the process of analyzing whether we should move in that direction or not. All of our programs have been developed this way.

We just developed over the last year a master's and an undergraduate degree in e-business, and the whole process was done hand-in-hand with the employers who are absolutely central to the success of such a program. Our programs didn't just come out of thin air.

So few of us have the resources that you have as a for-profit. When you say you do very extensive and expensive assessments beforehand, how do you do them?

Do you hire research firms? Do you have in-house assessment folks who do this?

This kind of research usually begins within our own institutional research office. We have somewhere between twenty-five and thirty people working on institutional research issues, perhaps the largest institutional research group of any university. Their job is to do environmental scans as well as internal assessments.

In many cases, our staff isn't large enough to do certain kinds of analyses, so we outsource those. When we come to Charlotte, for example, we will know a lot about Charlotte beforehand and we will do a fairly extensive market study. We will also work with our campuses in the nearby region and help fill them in on things we've discovered about Charlotte. We're not always capable of doing that in geographic areas where we don't already have our people nearby.

When we outsource studies, we crosscheck them. We put them through our own wringer to see if the findings really make sense, based on comparative analyses with other similarly situated areas.

Focus groups are another expense. We use focus groups for practically everything we do.

Remember that this all stems from our philosophy: If you're not measuring it or assessing it in some fashion, how would you know what policy to create around it? How would you know what decision to make? If anyone at the University says, "Oh no, we can't do that for this reason," the first response of everyone else is, "Show me the data," because we have data on just about everything of relevance to us.

How does the University of Phoenix assess student learning?

While we focus on trying to do everything possible for students to have access to higher education, we do have a series of minimum standards that students must be able to meet in order to enter our undergraduate or graduate programs.

Once a student meets our entrance requirements and enrolls, the student will begin his or her academic career at the University of Phoenix with a three-hour cognitive and affective assessment exam. We begin by assessing the students' cognitive knowledge of the field they plan to study. Because we focus on practical skills — that's why students come to us — we also assess them on critical thinking, communications skills, and those affective traits and qualities that are assumed to be key to success in their career. As a consequence, according to some researchers at Educational Testing Service (ETS), we have the largest database on adult education in the United States.

Every single student is then assessed on the same things when he or she graduates: cognitive knowledge, affective traits, critical-thinking skills, and communications skills. In this way, we make sure that the money they spend going to the University of Phoenix and the time that they took away from their spouses, dogs, employers, and children was well spent, with a significant return on their (and for many, their employers') investment. We can bring that information directly to the students and their employers. (Keep in mind that we work as closely with employers as with our students. That's how we create effective systems

and relevant curricula.)

We also want to know how our students are doing compared with their peers in other systems. We therefore use the ETS's Major Field Tests and Graduate Management Admissions Test (GMAT).

While our aim is to have all our students take comprehensive exams at the beginning and end of their academic career, not all fields have national exams at this time. Many of our students are in our MBA programs, for example, and there's no national exam for an MBA today. Even in those programs for which national exams do exist, we ordinarily can't compare apples with apples, meaning our employed adult students against employed adult students in other systems.

A big part of what we're doing with assessment, therefore, is working with ETS and others to address the need for meaningful comparisons between our database and those of others in traditional settings. We need to create a national norming structure for adult students and to develop new comprehensive exams that ETS can market elsewhere. Our critical-thinking assessments, for example, draw a lot from both nationally normed exams and our own work. While we are beginning some of this collaborative work with ETS, I can't guarantee that we'll work with them exclusively as opposed to other testing services.

How do you get your seniors to show up to take a three-hour test? And how do you guarantee that they'll take the test seriously?

These are questions that continually vex us. We have not overcome human nature. We are learning that if you really want to pull off a post-test, it must be hidden from the students. We therefore embed it into other activities so they no longer know when it's hitting them. It may be structured, for instance, into their last two courses, or it may be divided up in some other way so that they cannot tell whether they have finished, say, the critical-thinking part of the exam. As a consequence of embedding post-test assessments into coursework, the assessments become "high-stakes" because they're counted toward the course grade.

Another thing we have done, in order to assess continually even the post-test process, is to pay some students to take the exam. This gives us a constant benchmarking of students who really pay attention to doing the best they can on the exam against those who take the embedded exam. This is an example of the redundancy of our assessment system — purposely so because assessment is such a complex affair.

One of the hallmarks of the American higher education system has been our lack of standardization — our free-wheeling, creative approach. With your talk of a single national exam and standardization of the curriculum, should we worry about automatons teaching at the University of Phoenix?

Well, all of us should always worry about automatons at any institution. But here's my immediate response. Everywhere there are some faculty members who are really, really good. They do everything that we dream about when we think about the ideal of a terrific education. But we all know that they're very rare.

So at the University of Phoenix we have attempted to bring all our courses up to the level of those ideal courses. We're not a faculty-centered institution; we're a student-centered institution. Therefore, we do not want the quality of a student's education to depend on the whim of the teacher on a particular day. We do not want the quality of a student's education to suffer because he or she unfortunately can only take a course at a particular time on a particular day when an idiot is teaching it, and when everybody knows the best professor is teaching the same course three hours later or on another day.

We wanted to remove those luck-of-the-draw impediments to a quality education. We also don't want to leave the burden of creating the curriculum on the shoulders of one individual professor, however good he or she may be. So we have set up a faculty governance structure with broad input and with as uniform a quality as possible. (Again, it's all dependent on massive assessment and quality control processes.)

But the struggle to create a quality education across an entire system does come with a price. Part of the price is that some faculty, until they get the hang of it, might very well feel that if they could have taught their course differently, it would have been much better.

What we ask such faculty to do is make a formal suggestion to change the curriculum. If a faculty member thinks, for example, that we're using a miserable case study and there's a better one, it is his or her responsibility to make that suggestion. The suggestion goes to campus subject matter (disciplinary) curriculum committees, through campus-level curriculum committees, all the way up to the University's academic council. If these groups think it's a good idea, it becomes a part of the course. But if you are the only person who thinks your case is better, and everyone else teaching it across the United States thinks you're nuts, we're not going to change our curriculum no matter how creative your approach is.

So what you are saying then is that while your learning-centered, assessment-based approach gives a few less degrees of freedom for flexibility for faculty, faculty can still use their disciplinary expertise and deliver through a process by which students really learn.

Yes. What is really uniform about the University of Phoenix is not so much the content of the curriculum as the assessment mechanisms we use to make sure our students achieve stated outcomes. As I've told some faculty members, if you can teach accounting better with the poetry of Emily Dickinson, do it. I will know whether you managed to pull it off or not.

How are students assessed in their coursework?

Our students are assessed continually, through every course, not only in terms of what they do in the classroom, but also in terms of what they do in the study group or section meeting that is a required component of every course in every program.

In section meetings, students work in groups to develop group projects, to learn to interact, and to develop enough focus to be able to do their share of the group's work. The students work on their own, for the most part, but the faculty member must be accessible to them. We are now beginning to create electronic logs that students must maintain as they work through the study group process.

How do you view "seat time" at the University of Phoenix?

"Seat time" is the idea that unless you've got your rear on a seat for a certain number of hours, you're not going to learn. It has its advocates despite the fact that absolutely nothing is put in place to force any assessment that learning actually takes place as a consequence of mere time spent on task.

This is a topic that exercises me a great deal. Until very, very recently the focus of accreditation was on seat time, and it's still at the heart of U.S. Department of Education thinking. Probably no struggle between the University of Phoenix and regulators has been more intense than the issue of seat time. It's somewhat ironic, because our students have to sit in seats longer than most other students do. When we say "an hour" of class, we mean sixty minutes, not forty-five or fifty.

The focus on the seat time issue thwarts all of us from providing the best education that we want to make possible. The University of Phoenix's focus has been on creating a curriculum that is completely outcomes-based and on assessing those outcomes. This focus gives us the freedom to create the flexible structures necessary to be able to provide the education our students want and need.

But an outcomes-based model also requires us to have an assessment system that demonstrates that we are indeed achieving what we claim we are.

Very high levels of assessment are necessary to address the very high levels of accountability that come with the removal of input-oriented notions such as Carnegie units or seat time.

What about assessments at the program level?

To make sure that we don't just assess student performance, we have a series of assessments for our programs as well. In addition to the comparative exams I described earlier, on a regular basis we bring in reviewers from other universities to rigorously analyze each program and make sure it is structured to do what it's supposed to be doing at the proper level of rigor.

Libraries and information literacy are areas of increasing tension between you and accreditors. How do you measure outcomes in those areas?

We are working our way through that, but we are now integrating information literacy at the beginning and at the end of our programs.

In order to give our students access to library resources, we have put together a huge online library structure with adequate and continually up-to-date resources. As they work their way through that huge resource structure, our students develop an increasing self-understanding of how they come to realize what it is they don't know enough about. You can't search for information until you realize you need it but don't have it. So it's not just information literacy but a kind of ignorance training. We do a lot of ignorance training, trying to help our students understand what they don't know right now, so they can

go out and develop the right knowledge base and skills.

These skills are absolutely critical, I might add, because of our 75,500 students, 13,500 of them are doing all of their degree work online. We would like to see more and more students shifting to online education, because our online education is better for many of our students than is a seminar-based environment. Generally, our online students do better than our face-to-face students on our exams. So information (that is, IT) literacy is very significant for us.

Traditional non-profit colleges and universities hire faculty by looking, first and foremost, at the credential. If you have it, you go through a hiring process and then, boom, you're in the classroom to sink or swim.

The University of Phoenix uses a very different process to hire faculty, prepare them to teach, and assess their performance. What systems or strategies do you have in place to ensure that that part of the puzzle has quality? What do you do to recruit, train, orient, and also to retrain or keep your faculty?

The recruitment part is the result of a mixed bag, often people telling their friends and colleagues about opportunities at the University of Phoenix. Once recruited, our new faculty undergo about five weeks of training. About one out of every three or so doesn't make it through the process, because they really have to be able to teach. Not just teach, but teach adults who have more important things to do and have very little patience with incompetence.

After initial training, our faculty are assessed on a class-by-class basis. They are then periodically assessed at approximately six-month intervals and then annually. These reviews are done by the campus director of academic affairs and also by faculty peers. If our faculty are not making it at some point, we put resources into them to try and get them up to speed. If they still can't do it, they're just not rehired to teach.

We use a fairly extensive end-of-course student survey as part of this process. It doesn't ask typical questions, such as whether you liked the professor or would recommend the course to someone else, because that's not our main concern. The real issue is whether the course and the rest of the system worked for the student. Was the faculty member and the curriculum appropriate? Were the financial aid services appropriate? Were other university services, such as admissions and the registrar process, appropriate?

At the end of every class, this survey gives us feedback not only on the course and the professor but also on our entire system.

You can see, then, that we don't view assessments of students, programs, and faculty as separate matters. All of our assessments are part of a system with layers of continual assessments about everything that contributes to the learning and education process. We have weekly, monthly, quarterly, and ultimately annual reports. We have consolidated reports not only for the entire university but also for faculty member by faculty member, campus by campus, and program within a campus by program within a campus. This gives us a series of benchmarks. We can tell when a particular program is not doing well in a particular campus, because we can compare it against the same program on other campuses.

We build in a tremendous amount of redundancy in our assessments to make sure that the quality of our education is consistent, whether you're taking a course in St. Petersburg, Florida, in Detroit, in the Netherlands, or in San Jose, California.

Was it a challenge to achieve regional accreditation through the North Central Association (NCA)?

Although we fought tooth and nail with the NCA through the accreditation process, because of it we learned a tremendous amount about how we do what we do and how to come to do it better. I think most institutions don't appreciate how much they can learn from their fellow institutions through the process of accreditation.

Jorge Klor de Alva, former president of the University of Phoenix, is president and chief executive officer of Apollo International, the University's parent company; he is a member of the AAHE Board of Directors. Gail Mellow is president of LaGuardia College, and also is a member of the AAHE Board.

Promoting Deep Learning Through Teaching and Assessment

by Noel Entwistle

In order to be useful, research into teaching and learning needs to conceptualize not only the types of learning we wish to encourage but also the types of teaching-learning environments that are most likely to encourage and support such learning. Those of us involved in research on student learning believe we have a framework that does just that. Research in Sweden, Britain, and other countries has led to new ways of thinking about how teaching and assessment in higher education influence the quality of student learning. We have developed a framework of concepts and categories for teaching and learning that makes new ideas readily accessible to faculty members.

Research From the Student's Perspective

Research on student learning has sought to portray the experiences of both students and faculty. The starting point was to describe the main differences in how students think about learning and carry out their studying.

Research has been carried out on two fronts. On one front, through interviews with students, we studied what students believe learning involves and how they go about tasks such as reading articles or writing essays. The interviews have generally encouraged students not just to report their ways of tackling academic tasks, but also to reflect on their approaches. In analyzing the interview transcripts, we have used a rigorous procedure to establish categories and the relationship between those categories, a technique that contributes to a research approach described as *phenomenography* (Marton 1994).

The second line of development in research on student learning has been to design instruments to measure these concepts and so study larger groups of students. The *Approaches to Studying Inventory* and its more recent version (*ASSIST*) include sub-scales that cover the categories found from the interviews. We have used factor analysis of the sub-scales to refine our definitions of the categories (e.g., Biggs 1987; Entwistle & Ramsden 1983).

These two complementary approaches have established how teaching and assessment influence both how students study and the level of understanding they reach. This is what will be discussed here.

Conceptions of Learning and Approaches to Studying

When adults were asked, "What do you mean by 'learning'?" they had very different conceptions (Säljö 1979; Marton & Säljö 1997) that fell into a hierarchy that parallels the development of students' thinking as identified by Perry (1970). Some students see learning as mainly a matter of memorizing and *reproducing* knowledge in ways acceptable to the teacher. Others see learning as a way to establish personal meaning, by *transforming* the incoming information and ideas in relation to their existing knowledge and experience.

The conception of learning that students hold substantially affects how they tackle everyday academic tasks, and that brings us to a key concept that describes students' approaches to learning and studying. In an investigation of how students went about reading (Marton & Säljö 1976), students were asked to read an academic article and were told that they would be asked questions on it afterwards. It became clear that students interpreted this instruction very differently, and their ability to answer questions about the meaning of the text depended on how they decided to tackle the task. Some students sought a thorough understanding of the author's message, while others relied on "question-spotting" — learning just those pieces of information expected to come up in the test.

This distinction was gradually refined to produce the concept of *deep and surface approaches* to learning.

In the *deep* approach, the student intends to understand ideas for himself or herself. Such a student learns by *actively transforming*. Deep learners:

- Relate ideas to previous knowledge and experience;
- Look for patterns and underlying principles;
- Check evidence and relate it to conclusions;
- Examine logic and argument cautiously and critically;
- Are aware of the understanding that develops while learning; and
- Become actively interested in the course content.

In the *surface* approach, the student intends merely to cope with course requirements in a minimalist fashion. Such a student learns by *passively reproducing*. Surface learners:

- Treat the course as unrelated bits of knowledge;
- Memorize facts and carry out procedures routinely;
- Find difficulty in making sense of new ideas presented;
- See little value or meaning in either courses or tasks;
- Study without reflecting on either purpose or strategy; and
- Feel undue pressure and worry about work.

These two approaches to learning can

be illustrated through the contrasting responses of two engineering students asked about their ways of studying:

Interviewer: Tell me something about how are you tackling this course and how you work on the problem sheets you are given.

Surface Approach: *I suppose I'm mainly concerned about being able to remember all the important facts and theories that we've been given in the lectures. We are given an awful lot of stuff to learn, so I just plough through it as best I can. I try to take it all down in the lectures, and then go over it until I'm sure they won't catch me out in the exams. . . . [With the problem sheets], the first step is to decide which part of the lecture course the problem comes from. Then I look through my notes until I find an example that looks similar, and I try it out. Basically, I just apply the formula and see if it works. If it doesn't, I look for another example, and try a different formula. Usually it's fairly obvious which formula fits the problem, but sometimes it doesn't seem to work out, and then I'm really stuck.*

Deep Approach: *It is not easy, you know. There is a great deal to cover, and I am not satisfied unless I really understand what we're given. I take quite full notes, but afterwards I go through them and check on things that I'm not clear about. I find that working through the problem sheets we're given is a good way to test whether I know how to apply the theory covered in lectures, and I do that regularly. Once you realize what lies behind the problems — that's the physics of it and what makes it a problem — then you can do them. You get a kick out of it too, when it all begins to make sense. Applying the right formula is not difficult, once you know you are on the right lines.*

Interviews on studying have also drawn attention to the pervasive influence of assessment procedures on learning and studying. Research has identified a third category — the *strategic* approach — in which the student intends to achieve the highest possible grades. Such a student learns by *reflectively organizing*. Strategic learners:

- Put consistent effort into studying;
- Manage time and effort effectively;
- Find the right conditions and materials for studying;
- Monitor the effectiveness of ways of studying;
- Are alert to assessment requirements and criteria; and
- Gear work to the perceived preferences of the teacher.

The strategic approach can be seen in the comments of this student (Miller & Parlett 1974):

I play the examination game. The examiners play it, so we play it too. . . . The technique involves knowing what's going to be in the exam and how it's going to be marked. You can acquire these techniques from sitting in a lecturer's class, getting ideas from his point of view, the form of his notes, and the books he has written — and this is separate to picking up the actual work content.

This quotation suggests a student

concerned with both academic content and the demands of the assessment system. The interest in the content is typical of a deep approach, but the alertness to assessment requirements is strategic.

Subsequent research using the *Approaches to Studying Inventory* and *ASSIST* has found that these three broad factors can be further reduced into a single description of an idealized approach to studying that combines deep and strategic and excludes any elements of the surface apathetic (Entwistle, McCune & Walker 2000). Several studies have confirmed that the deep strategic approach leads to higher grades, but only where the assessment actually requires understanding to be demonstrated (see Entwistle 2000).

There are important caveats, however, in using these categories:

1. They can only be used to describe the relative prominence of each approach to studying in any student. It is wrong to try to put any student wholly into any one category.

2. The categories are broad, indicative labels that do not do justice to the complex individual ways that students study (McCune 1998; Entwistle, McCune & Walker 2000).

3. The processes needed to develop deep learning will vary between subject areas. Because approaches depend on context and the content and only partly reflect a habitual way of studying, an approach can be applied with any confidence only to a particular course, or even a specific occasion.

Outcomes of Learning

There seems to be widespread agreement among most higher education practitioners that one of our main aims is to encourage the development of complex conceptual understanding, particularly what has been described as "critical thinking" (Entwistle 1997).

Students do not develop such understanding quickly or easily, so this type of thinking is only acquired gradually over the student's academic career. If we are to help students recognize the importance of developing complex conceptual understanding, we must be able to identify, and reward, different levels of understanding.

Through interviews with final-year students at Edinburgh, we have been able to build on earlier research (summarized in Biggs 1999) to identify five levels of understanding that students reach as outcomes of learning (Entwistle 1995; Entwistle & Entwistle 1997; Entwistle 2000):

*   *Mentioning:* incoherent bits of information without any obvious structure;
*   *Describing:* brief descriptions of topics derived mainly from material provided;
*   *Relating:* an outline with personal explanations, lacking in detail or supporting arguments;
*   *Explaining:* relevant evidence used to develop structured, independent arguments; and
*   *Conceiving:* individual conceptions of topics developed through reflection.

Other analyses of the Edinburgh interviews have explored students' experiences in reaching deep levels of understanding. Students find the experience is emotionally satisfying. The understanding they construct carries a feeling of "provisional wholeness" — complete for the time being, but still to be developed further. Typical student comments have yielded the following composite description of the experience of understanding:

> *Understanding is the interconnection of lots of disparate things . . . the feeling that you understand how the whole thing is connected up — you can make sense of it internally. . . . If I don't understand, it's just everything floating about and you can't quite get everything into place — like jigsaw pieces, you know, suddenly connect and you can see the whole picture. . . . But there is always the feeling you can add more and more and more. . . . [Understanding], well, for me, it's when I . . . could explain it so that I felt satisfied with the explanation. . . . [When you understand like that] you can't not understand it [afterwards]. You can't 'de-understand' it!*

Several students in our study experienced this sense of connection visually, through their revision notes. This suggests that they were conscious of the structure of their understanding and could review it, re-orient it, and use it to pull in supportive details believed to be "stored separately." Their sense of structure gave them a logical pathway to guide the emerging structure of an essay. They could adapt this pathway as it developed to match the requirements of the question (Entwistle 1998a).

We have described this direct experience of understanding as a *knowledge object* (Entwistle & Marton 1994). Once firmly established, it seems to be resilient and potentially long-lasting in the memory, although retrieval may depend on the availability of strong cues.

The idea of a knowledge object and its functions can be illustrated through two quotations from students on how they prepare for and take essay examinations (Entwistle 1995; Entwistle & Entwistle 1997). The visual aspect comes out clearly in the first quotation, while the second shows the way in which the student monitored the process.

> ***First Student***: *I can see that virtually as a picture, and I can review it, and bring in more facts about each part. . . . Looking at a particular part of the diagram sort of triggers off other thoughts. I find schematics, in flow diagrams and the like, very useful because a schematic acts a bit like a syllabus; it tells you what you should know, without actually telling you what it is. I think the facts are stored separately, . . . and the schematic is like an index, I suppose.*

> ***Second Student***: *The more I have done exams, the more I'd liken them to a performance, like being on a stage; . . . having not so much to present the fact that you know a vast amount, but having to perform well with what you do know — sort of playing to the gallery. . . . I was very conscious of being outside what I was writing.*

Two more quotations indicate the flexibility of the knowledge object and how its existence is experienced as being almost independent.

[My way of preparing for the exam] gave you quite a broad base from which to answer any question that came up on that topic, so you were used to being flexible in the way that you answered the question. It allowed you to adapt to different ways in which the question could be worded, and it also organized in your mind the relationships between different aspects of, and approaches to, a question.

Following that logic through, it pulls in pictures and facts as it needs them. . . . Each time I describe [a particular topic], it's likely to be different. . . . Well, you start with evolution, say, . . . and suddenly you know where you're going next. Then, you might have a choice . . . to go in that direction or that direction . . . and follow it through various options it's offering. . . . Hopefully, you'll make the right choice, and so this goes to this, goes to this — and you've explained it to the level you've got to. Then, it says "Okay, you can go on to talk about further criticisms in the time you've got left."

Conceptions of Teaching

Research has suggested not only a hierarchy of conceptions of learning but also a hierarchy of conceptions of teaching. Researchers have asked faculty members to describe what they mean by "learning" and "teaching" and to share their beliefs about teaching and assessment (Prosser, Trigwell & Taylor 1994; Van Driel et al. 1997; Kember 1998). The three main categories that have emerged closely parallel in underlying meaning those found by Säljö

and by Perry for student conceptions of learning.

Some faculty, those we call *teacher-focused* and *content-oriented*, talk about the importance of covering the syllabus and ensuring that students acquire the correct information and ideas. A second, smaller group, *focusing on student activity*, provide assignments designed to ensure active learning and help students develop effective study skills, but they still see learning in their own terms. We call the final group, smallest of the three, *student-focused* and *learning-oriented*. Such faculty are most concerned with helping students to develop personal understanding and more sophisticated conceptions, and they design their teaching and assessment accordingly.

Again, examples from the interviews may help to clarify the two extreme categories:

Teacher-Focused and Content-Oriented: It is my duty and responsibility to help students develop the specific knowledge and skills which are needed to pass the examinations, although I'm fully aware that this might narrow the kind of education I'm giving the students. . . . I put great emphasis on objectives and making sure that I cover the syllabus thoroughly. In preparing a lecture, . . . I know exactly what notes I want the students to get. Students don't have to decide when to take notes: I dictate them.

Student-Focused and Learning-Oriented: I'm aware of how much I used to assume. I now try to take nothing for granted and to question my assumptions about how students learn things. . . . What I want to achieve is confronting students with their preconceived ideas about the subject. . . . [Conceptual understanding is developed] by arguing about things and trying to apply ideas. . . . What we're trying to do is . . . to shift [students] from the layperson's view, to what we would call a scientific . . . [or academic] view.

Teachers with these contrasting conceptions of teaching tend to hold corresponding views on their students and assessment procedures. Teacher-focused faculty are likely to see assessment as designed to demonstrate detailed factual knowledge of the syllabus. They tend to consider learning outcomes as being almost entirely the responsibility of the students themselves, depending on ability and motivation. Student-focused faculty, on the other hand, tend to use more varied methods of assessment and to be aware of their own responsibility for encouraging students to develop deep levels of understanding.

Promoting Deep Learning

A wide range of studies over the last twenty-five years have established how teaching, assessment, and other aspects of the learning environment affect students' approaches to studying and thus the quality of learning outcomes.

Seven aspects of lecturing have often been described as "good teaching." Four of them — clarity, level, pace, and structure — are all important in conveying information. *Clarity* describes audibility and visibility but has also

been used to describe a more general quality in teaching. *Level* indicates that the lecturer is aware of the students' current level of understanding and designs his or her teaching to match it; *structure* relates to the way in which the content of the lecture has been organized to bring out its logical framework.

The other three aspects — explanation, enthusiasm, and empathy — seem to have the strongest effect on deep learning (Entwistle 1998b, 2000). The quality of the *explanation* determines how easy it is for students to understand the content; *enthusiasm* arouses interest and motivates learning. *Empathy* describes the emotional climate the teacher develops, which powerfully affects the willingness with which students engage with the ideas presented.

While we have a clear idea of how to influence levels of understanding, there are still great difficulties in achieving this ideal in practice (see Hounsell 1997). Linking the ideas of Eizenberg (1988), Wiske (1998), and more general literature on student learning, we reach the following conclusions:

First, deep learning can be promoted through *curriculum design* by
- Identifying generative, open topics;
- Using aims to emphasize understanding;
- Incorporating authentic, relevant topics;
- Defining "essential" information; and
- Selecting appropriate textbooks.

Second, deep learning can be promoted through *teaching* by

- Analyzing the derivation of new terms;
- Emphasizing principles and concepts;
- Conveying information effectively (through clarity, level, pace, and structure); and
- Evoking a deep response (through explanation, enthusiasm, and empathy).

Finally, deep learning can be promoted through *assessment* by
- Focusing on understanding performance, using tasks to develop and demonstrate understanding and feedback to clarify and stress understanding;
- Using techniques to tap understanding, including more open-ended questions and less reliance on multiple-choice questions; and
- Grading in relation to levels of understanding, using qualitative criteria to boost validity.

The influence of assessment on deep learning is clear-cut. Assessment techniques that encourage students to think for themselves — such as essay questions, applications to new contexts, and problem-based questions — all shift students toward a deep approach. Assessment perceived by students as requiring no more than the accurate reproduction of information lets students rely on a surface approach.

Multiple-choice questions and short-answer questions are the worst offenders (Thomas & Bain 1984; Scouller 1998). Although multiple-choice questions can, of course, be written to test understanding, the vast majority of tests written by faculty require mainly factual knowledge (Milton, Pollio & Ei-

son 1982). Gardiner (1994) concluded that most faculty members do not have the expertise to develop multiple-choice questions that test higher-level thinking skills, and yet this technique is widely used to cope with large undergraduate classes. With our emphasis on ease and accuracy of marking, we seem to have lost sight of the way assessment controls the form of learning that students undertake (Scouller 1998).

This draws attention to the influence of students' perceptions on their learning. It is not the teaching-learning environment itself that determines approaches to studying, but rather what students believe to be required. Those perceptions come from the comments of faculty and teaching assistants, during their teaching and when marking term papers, from previous tests or examination papers, and also from discussions with other students.

There are also wide differences in how students interpret and make use of their learning environment (Meyer 1991). Students with a deep strategic approach are much more likely to recognize and make use of the opportunities for deep learning provided within the learning environment. Less well-prepared students, who need the most support, seem less able to recognize or use the support that is offered (Vermunt & Meyer 2000).

Learning outcomes are affected not only by student approaches to learning and faculty approaches to teaching and assessment but also by department and institutional policies and procedures (Entwistle 1998b), including departmental teaching ethos, course design and objectives, feedback to students, assessment procedures, freedom of choice, workload, study skill support, learning materials, and library provisions. The interaction among these three elements — students, faculty, and organizational environment — is complex.

Conclusion

Depth of learning is affected by the cognitive processes students use. These processes are, in turn, affected by student conceptions of learning (what students believe learning requires of them) and their approaches to studying (strategic or apathetic). Only by using appropriate cognitive processes can a deep level of understanding be achieved.

But such understanding does not solely depend on the student. Faculty also differ in their conception of learning, which affects their teaching and assessment methods and their attitudes toward students. The way in which faculty set up and operate the teaching-learning environment affects their students' balance between deep and surface approaches, and so the quality of learning outcomes achieved.

The following summarizes some of the main ways research suggests we can improve deep learning.

- Provide overarching goals, generative topics, and clear aims.
- Relate teaching directly to prior knowledge.
- Teach so as to clarify meanings and arouse interest.
- Encourage metacognitive alertness and self-regulation in studying.
- Introduce formative assessments designed to develop understanding.
- Develop marking criteria to describe levels of understanding.
- Use assessment techniques that encourage and reward conceptual understanding.

How these guidelines are implemented depends, of course, on the subject area, the course objectives, and the composition of the class. How effectively these principles are implemented thus depends on the professional judgement and insight of faculty members.

References

Biggs, J.B. (1987). *Student Approaches to Learning and Studying.* Melbourne, Australia: Australian Council for Educational Research.

———. (1999). *Teaching for Quality Learning at University.* Buckingham, England: Open University Press.

Eizenberg, N. (1988). "Approaches to Learning Anatomy: Developing a Programme for Pre-Clinical Medical Students." In P. Ramsden (Ed.), *Improving Learning: New Perspectives* (pp. 178-198). London: Kogan Page.

Entwistle, N.J. (1995). "Frameworks for Understanding as Experienced in Essay Writing and in Preparing for Examinations." *Educational Psychologist, 30:* 47-54.

———. (1997). "Contrasting Perspectives on Learning." In F. Marton, D.J. Hounsell & N.J. Entwistle (Eds.), *The Experience of Learning* (2nd ed., pp. 3-22). Edinburgh, Scotland: Scottish Academic Press.

———. (1998a). "Approaches to Learning and Forms of Understanding." In B. Dart & G. Boulton-Lewis (Eds.), *Teaching and Learning in Higher Education* (pp. 72-101). Melbourne, Australia: Australian Council for Educational Research.

——— . (1998b). "Improving Teaching Through Research on Student Learning." In J.J.F. Forest (Ed.), *University Teaching: International Perspectives* (pp. 73-112). New York: Garland.

——— . (2000). "Approaches to Studying and Levels of Understanding: The Influences of Teaching and Assessment." In J.C. Smart (Ed.), *Higher Education: Handbook of Theory and Research: Vol. 15* (pp. 156-218). New York: Agathon Press.

——— , & Entwistle, A.C. (1997). "Revision and the Experience of Understanding." In F. Marton, D.J. Hounsell & N.J. Entwistle (Eds.), *The Experience of Learning* (2nd ed., pp. 145-158). Edinburgh, Scotland: Scottish Academic Press.

Entwistle, N.J., & Marton, F. (1994). "Knowledge Objects: Understandings Constituted Through Intensive Academic Study." *British Journal of Educational Psychology, 64:* 161-178.

Entwistle, N.J., McCune, V., & Walker, P. (2000). "Conceptions, Styles and Approaches Within Higher Education: Analytic Abstractions and Everyday Experience." In R.J. Sternberg & L-F. Zhang (Eds.), *Perspectives on Cognitive, Learning, and Thinking Styles.* Mahwah, NJ: Lawrence Erlbaum.

Entwistle, N.J., & Ramsden, P. (1983). *Understanding Student Learning.* London: Croom Helm.

Gardiner, L.F. (1994). *Redesigning Higher Education* (ASHE-ERIC Higher Education Reports). Washington: George Washington University, Graduate School of Education and Human Development.

Hounsell, D.J. (1997). "Understanding Teaching and Teaching for Understanding." In F. Marton, D.J. Hounsell & N.J. Entwistle (Eds.), *The Experience of Learning* (2nd ed., pp. 39-58). Edinburgh, Scotland: Scottish Academic Press.

Kember, D. (1998). "Teaching Beliefs and Their Impact on Students' Approach to Learning." In B. Dart & G. Boulton-Lewis (Eds.), *Teaching and Learning in Higher Education* (pp. 1-25). Melbourne, Australia: Australian Council for Educational Research.

Marton, F. (1994). "Phenomenography." In T. Husen and N. Postlethwaite (Eds.), *International Encyclopedia of Education* (pp. 4424-4429). Oxford, England: Pergamon.

Marton, F., & Säljö, R. (1976). "On Qualitative Differences in Learning. I. Outcome and Process." *British Journal of Educational Psychology, 46:* 4-11.

——— . (1997). "Approaches to Learning." In F. Marton, D.J. Hounsell & N.J. Entwistle (Eds.), *The Experience of Learning* (2nd ed.). Edinburgh, Scotland: Scottish Academic Press.

McCune, V. (1998). "Academic Development During the First Year at University." In C. Rust (Ed.), *Improving Students as Learners* (pp. 354-358). Oxford, England: Oxford Brookes University, Centre for Staff and Learning Development.

Meyer, J.H.F. (1991). "Study Orchestration: The Manifestation, Interpretation and Consequences of Contextualised Approaches to Studying." *Higher Education, 22:* 297-316.

Miller, C.M.L., & Parlett, M. (1974). *Up to the Mark: A Study of the Examination Game.* London: Society for Research in Higher Education.

Milton, O., Pollio, H.R. & Eison, J.A. (1982). *Making Sense of College Grades.* San Francisco: Jossey-Bass.

Perry, W.G. (1970). *Forms of Intellectual and Ethical Development in the College Years: A Scheme.* New York: Holt, Rinehart & Winston.

Prosser, M., Trigwell, K., & Taylor, P. (1994). "A Phenomenographic Study of Academics' Conceptions of Science Learning and Teaching." *Learning & Instruction, 4:* 217-232.

Säljö, R. (1979). *Learning in the Learner's Perspective: Vol. I. Some Common-Sense Conceptions* (Report 76). Gothenburg, Sweden: University of Gothenburg, Department of Education.

Scouller, K. (1998). "The Influence of Assessment Method on Students' Learning Approaches: Multiple Choice Question Examination Versus Assignment Essay." *Higher Education, 35:* 453-452.

Thomas, P.R., & Bain, J.D. (1984). "Contextual Dependence of Learning Approaches: The Effects of Assessments." *Human Learning, 3:* 227-240.

Van Driel, J.H., Verloop, N., Van Werven, H.I., & Dekkers, H. (1997). "Teachers' Craft Knowledge and Curriculum Innovation in Higher Engineering Education." *Higher Education, 34:* 105-122.

Vermunt, J., & Meyer, J.H.F. (2000). "Dissonant Study Orchestration." *European Journal of the Psychology of Education* (whole issue).

Wiske M.S. (Ed.). (1998). *Teaching for Understanding: Linking Research With Practice.* San Francisco: Jossey-Bass.

Noel Entwistle is Bell Professor of Education at the University of Edinburgh, in Scotland.

Developing a Learning/Teaching Style Assessment Model for Diverse Populations

by James Anderson

Scenario One: At a regional community college, a non-traditional adult student has experienced discomfort in most of her classes. While she listens to the rapid responses of her classmates — traditional 18-to-22-year-olds — she has difficulty with the abstract nature of the course content and the examples the other students use. The non-traditional student also has anxieties about her readiness for college. How can the instructor better meet her needs?

Scenario Two: At a Midwestern university, "technology in the classroom" has become the new mantra. Decisions about hardware and software do not follow a consistent pattern. High-performance and well-skilled students exhibit learning preferences that match the instructional styles of the university's highly analytical faculty. Average and less-skilled students are not yet at the level of analytical excellence that

would facilitate their success. Their technology needs are different, and they prefer a different mode of classroom instruction, both with and without technology. What can be done for them?

Scenario Three: At many institutions, faculty call for a "better" student to be admitted, one who can perform better, write better, think better, is more motivated, etc. Even when their institution's mission is to admit a broad range of students, such faculty still describe "quality" in terms of high-end, well-skilled students with whom the faculty are comfortable. At other institutions with the same mission, same type of student, and same approach to quality, however, their faculty promote success among all incoming students. At these institutions, faculty are student-centered in terms of their teaching. What does this really mean?

Scenario Four: The new Director of Disability Services suggests to the Vice

President for Academic Affairs that the institution change the focus of its faculty-development initiatives on accommodating students whose disability interferes with their ability to process information (via lecture, text, etc.). The Director's argument is that altering teaching style would best serve the needs of such students. But faculty counter that they already offer extended testing time for students who are disabled. Is the Director demanding too much?

All these scenarios point to the need for us to understand learning styles, relate them to diverse needs, and design appropriate assessments for them.

What are learning styles? "Learning style" refers to the preferred manner in which an individual or group assimilates, organizes, and uses information to make sense of the world, including a classroom or job environment.

Learning styles can be characterized by how we *prefer* to learn, specifically our preferences for:
- The type of information we receive (sensory vs. intuitive);
- How we perceive information (visual vs. verbal);
- How we organize information (inductive vs. deductive);
- How we process information (actively vs. reflectively); and
- How we understand information (sequentially vs. globally).

There are many dimensions of learning styles, including:
- Reflective vs. Impulsive
- Non-affective vs. Affective
- Elaborative vs. Shallow (repetitive) processing
- Scanning (visual) vs. Focusing
- Field-independent vs. Field-sensitive
- Analytical vs. Relational
- Independent vs. Dependent
- Participant vs. Avoidant

An Example: Analytical and Relational Learners

An analytical learner is able to dis-embed information from the total picture and focus on details. As analytical learners listen to a speaker or look at a slide, in microseconds they process everything they're absorbing against what they've already stored. As they do this, they dis-embed information that doesn't agree with what they already think or need to know.

Analytical learners think sequentially and structurally. They:
- Can learn inanimate and impersonal material;
- Don't need to hear examples that they can literally reach out and touch in terms of cultural or experiential relevance;
- Have a good memory for irrelevant and abstract information, such as calculus;
- Are very task-oriented; they can persist with unstimulating tasks;
- Do not let their performance be affected greatly by the opinions of others.

This style matches up with traditional educational environments, and such students are usually very successful academically.

Relational learners, at the other end of the continuum, prefer to look at information as a total picture, focusing on a gestalt rather than on details. They:
- Like to take it all in, because they need to make affective decisions

about the information (it's not that they are emotional learners; they want to understand cognitive, analytical information like everyone else does);

- Think improvisationally and intuitively;
- Prefer materials that have a human, social content and cultural relevance.
- Have a good memory for verbally presented ideas and information, especially if it is relevant to them;
- Tend to be more task-oriented in non-academic areas;
- Let their performance be influenced by expressions of confidence or doubt in their ability from authority figures;
- Prefer to withdraw from unstimulating tasks.

Relational learners have a processing mode that asks affective, personal, and social questions about information. If the information doesn't make sense in that context, if it doesn't come back with positive feedback, or if they don't see relevance and familiarity in it, they lose interest in it. It's not that the information is not valuable; they just lose interest.

You can see that the relational learning style conflicts with traditional school environments, especially in scientific or technical fields. Think of the math courses you've taken in your life. How many teachers opened a lecture by saying, "By the end of class, you will understand how what I'm going to talk about today adapts to your personal life"? Relational learners can't get through tough, abstract bottlenecks such as Ohm's Law in electrical engineering, debits in accounting, vectors in physics, molecules in chemistry —

concepts for which we don't provide human/social content. Faculty will often ignore the needs of such relational learners, because faculty themselves are more analytical and task-oriented.

Another Example: Affective Learners

Affective students care about and evaluate the messenger as well as the message. They don't leave their affect outside the door. They may look at the instructor and say, "Boy, he sure is dressed funny today!" You and I would say, "What difference does that make?" but affective students focus on the social dynamics of the classroom. They value the instructor's presentation of self — i.e., whether the instructor immersed herself into the presentation and dialogue — as much as they value the presentation of ideas and content.

When I taught psychology courses, I always used my own life as an example, so my students could see the incorporation of self into my delivery of the content (except, that is, in abnormal psychology!). Affective learners want to convert what is abstract to something that has experiential, cultural relevancy. They like periodic feedback that tells them something about themselves as learners and connects to where they are as learners.

A Third Example: Visual Learners

Visual learners prefer to learn by scanning information from a lecture, text, or other source, searching for cues or focal points to which they can connect or relate.

We all engage in visual learning when we channel-surf late at night and scan channels for five seconds apiece.

We're looking for visual cues that tell us we should stay on a particular channel a little longer. In only a few seconds we decide, based on visual information, whether to stay or keep on channel-surfing.

Some students look at all the cues an instructor gives and select the most relevant information; others come primed to hear only the cues they want and ignore most other information. Some students prefer highly affective cues, which are examples that have relevancy and familiarity in terms of the student's experience.

If visual learners can't find such focal points, they focus on something else, and things begin to break down: They become bored or distracted. If students who are both visual and affective learners don't see a plethora of affective cues within three classes, they will tune out the instructor. They may not come to class. They may ask a friend to take notes. We know that a lot of dysfunctional things can happen when learning preferences are not accommodated early on.

When cues are provided for visual learners, however, their thinking is stimulated. They raise questions about the information. They want to pursue the subject more. The next step is almost imperceptible: They begin to draw on past experience to make the learning experience more holistic, more of a gestalt.

Why do some students need to read a chapter three or four times to get detail, and some need to read it only once? One reason is skill in pattern recognition. Every textbook chapter in every discipline has three components: details about the chapter's subject, explanations of the details, and example

of the explanations and details. Students who lack pattern recognition read all this together and can't distinguish details from explanations and examples. If you ask them a test question about a detail, they may provide an example instead. When they find out their answer is wrong, they'll ask, "Why is this wrong? It was in the book!"

Some visual learners lack skill in pattern recognition. Those who are skilled in pattern recognition can extract detail and separate it from example and explanation. Here's the key: They do this by drawing on past experience to develop the gestalt, a holistic perception of what's going on.

Once visual learners find cues and use them to create a holistic perception, they demonstrate goal-directed behavior: They study harder. They get in study groups. They raise questions in class. They see the instructor after class. When they read a chapter, they're more willing to think about pattern recognition.

Learning Styles as Continuums

I may have given the impression that learning styles fall into bipolar distributions — either students are visual learners or they're not, affective learners or they're not. In reality, learning styles are on continuums. We all have a learning style on each continuum, just in different places along the line. And there are instruments that allow us to identify where students are on these continuums.

Which learning styles are most effective? We have determined from research that students who are reflective, non-affective, elaborative-processing, scanning, field-independent, analytical learners are highly successful in both two-year and four-year colleges. They are our dream students. If they also come with a 1450 SAT and several Advanced Placement courses, their instructor can walk in every day and say anything, and they're going to get it. But in the real world, we want *all* our students to succeed, not just those primed for success.

An Evolving Discussion

The discussion of learning styles has not moved with the same impetus that many other discussions in higher education have. The discussion of learning communities, for example, has moved from a conceptual model to an implementation model; and discussions of teaching have moved to discussions of the scholarship of teaching. We have moved at warp speed in developing models for classroom assessment; but, again, we have not followed suit in developing assessment models that accommodate learning styles.

Why has the evolution of our ideas about learning styles moved at such a slow pace? I offer four reasons.

The first is that our conceptual models of learning styles have become locked into the places where they originated as research topics: cognitive psychology, visual perception, etc. Because they are locked in as research topics, they have not yet been applied significantly to teaching and learning at a practical, performance-based student level.

The second reason that our conceptual models of learning styles have not evolved is because we haven't connected them to classroom performance, writing, thinking, student success indicators, retention models, and so on. These connections do show up in the litera-

ture, but they're not an integral part of our dialogue.

The third reason is because many campuses are not yet student-centered. If a campus is lax in merely thinking about what good teaching is, and if it lacks a student-centered approach to teaching and learning, why would it want to examine student learning preferences, learning strategies, and learning styles?

The final reason I offer (and mine is not an exhaustive list) is because to discuss learning styles in earnest is ultimately to discuss differential performance of certain groups and the relationship between traditional teaching styles and the learning styles of diverse populations. Now we've moved from a research discussion to a *political* discussion. And if faculty don't want to address student-centered teaching, why would they want to address the politics of teaching and its connection to different groups?

Advancing the Conversation on the Needs of Diverse Learners

We all accept the notion that when we teach or engage in any type of academic support, not all our students have the same needs. All students have diverse needs that we want to meet. We want them to be better thinkers, better writers, better problem solvers, and so on.

Then there are particular groups of students who have unique needs that we also want to meet. Consider a returning adult who is less-skilled, raising a family and working full-time. If, because of poor advising, this student gets a full load of tough courses with abstract course content, he has a 100 percent chance of getting a D or F in almost every one of those courses.

So why haven't we looked out for the unique needs of certain diverse learners? One reason that diversity is not considered in many campus discussions of teaching, learning, assessment, scholarship, and research is that we ignore its natural fit with these endeavors. To see how easily diversity can be incorporated into discussions of learning style, recall how visual learners learn best: by drawing on personal, social, and cultural experiences to make the learning experience more holistic. By noting this, we have introduced diversity into the conversation on learning styles.

Cultural Differences in Learning Styles

When I began to study learning styles, the first thing I discovered was that there was no literature on group differences, with the exception of some work on differences in such things as visual perception, field independence, and field sensitivity. There were also some comparisons of Eurocentric groups with other groups — for example, Scottish children with Zambian children — but nothing connected to classroom performance, higher-order skills, etc.

But today we know a lot more. Do certain racial, ethnic, or cultural groups lean more toward some ends of the continuums than others do? Yes. Differences in learning styles are so pronounced that we can make clear distinctions among cultural groups, racial groups, gender groups, age groups, and so on. Students from certain groups tend to be disproportionately relational, affective learners. In the late 1980s, I leaned toward thinking there was something called a "Black Learning Style" or "Women's Learning Style."

But I've changed since then. If I could select two factors that probably have the most impact on students' learning styles and group differences, it would be *class* and *prior educational experiences,* be they in the family or in school. If you map the learning styles of whites in Appalachia and blacks in Mississippi, they'll look exactly alike. If you map the learning styles of students of color at Reed College in Oregon and at Harvard, again they'll map in similar ways . . . that is, bright, analytical students, regardless of race, will show up that way.

Some researchers are beginning to focus on a broader approach that identifies other dimensions of learning styles. Madge Willis (1989), for example, talks about learning styles of African-American children:

- *Social / Affective:* They tend to be people-oriented and emphasize the affective domain. Social interaction is crucial, and social learning is common.
- *Harmonious:* They tend to respect and encourage the interdependence and harmonic/communal aspects of people and environment. They seek knowledge for practical, utilitarian, and relevant purposes. They seek synthesis and holistic approaches to experiences.
- *Expressive Creativity:* They tend to be creative, adaptive, variable, novel, stylistic, and intuitive. They prefer simultaneous stimulation of multiple senses and oral expression.
- *Non-Verbal:* Non-verbal communication (intonation, body language, movement, and rhythm) are vital to helping these students learn.

Willis found that the response of diverse students in a classroom is affected by the following:

- They care about and evaluate the messenger (the instructor as well as the message). They value the instructor's presentation of self, as well as the presentation of ideas and content.
- They are concerned about the social dynamics of the class.
- They want abstract concepts converted into something that has experiential and/or cultural relevance or familiarity.
- They like periodic feedback that is aimed at the learner rather than the error, connects to the learner's developmental level, and focuses on what they can learn now.

Should We Encourage Students to Change Their Learning Style?

Students come to us with learning styles developed over many years, rooted in their culture, family background, and prior educational experiences. Do we want to go as far as I've suggested in studying group differences in learning styles? In doing so, are we suggesting that some groups are *deficient* in learning style? Of course not. We don't make evaluative judgments about learning styles; we affirm learning styles as a reflection of a student's heritage.

But should we nonetheless encourage some students to modify their learning style? Yes, because we live in the real world. The students who will be most successful in college move from the affective toward the analytical side. I look at the performance of affective students in tough courses, especially when they are dragging their affect into the classroom when it doesn't need to

be there — i.e., they can express their affect anywhere else, but in that classroom they need to be very focused.

It is not necessarily difficult to modify one's learning style. Most of us can move up and down these continuums, and we know exactly when we should do so. When we're in a restaurant with friends, for example, there's no need to have a highly analytical discussion about the caloric breakdown of everything that's on our plate or about the class differences among the people sitting around us. But if you're giving a conference presentation, you're going to move toward the analytical end of the continuum because you're addressing high-end, well-heeled learners.

We all have the jobs we have because we're good at this higher education thing. If there's one thing that we can share with students and help them learn, it's how to move up and down these continuums.

What about students who are highly analytical and devoid of affect? Don't they need to move to the affective side? Yes, they do at some point in life, but not necessarily while they're getting through college courses.

The Importance of Framing Questions

What are the implications of all this for each of us? If you want to develop an assessment model that addresses the needs of diverse populations, the most important thing that you can do is frame the questions that you want answered. What do you want to know? Why?

Here are some examples of framing questions to ask yourself:

- Do we seek only to identify students' attitudinal dispositions toward learning, without connecting them to teaching?

- Do we only want to know how students feel about learning and their learning preferences?
- Does our faculty have an understanding of general learning styles? (If we're at an open admissions institution, how can they not have an understanding, since every day in every class there is such a wide range of learners sitting in front of them across different dimensions, skill levels, learning styles, learning preferences, and motivational levels?)
- Who impacts faculty perceptions of student learning styles?
- Do we want to assess our students' learning styles? Whose responsibility is it to do this and get the information to faculty so they understand their students' needs?
- If we do collect such information, so what? What do we want to do with it?
- For those whom we identify as being most at risk for success, based on valid, objective information, what does it mean? What are we doing about it?
- How can we move less successful students incrementally through a process that allows them to become more successful? How do we move students from being affective to being more analytical?
- Should we adapt instructional styles to accommodate learning styles? What does that mean for faculty development? What does that mean for classroom assessment?
- What cognitive, affective, and cultural assets do diverse students bring to learning environments, and how do these assets facilitate or inhibit their performance? How can we tap into those assets?
- How do all aspects of diversity fit into assessing performance?
- To what degree do we want to assign students to sections according to styles and then match them up with certain instructors? Why should students who are less-skilled and affective learners be placed with a highly analytical instructor?
- Should we use information about learning styles to help students decide what to emphasize or de-emphasize in their studies? Students who take an entire semester online and who are highly verbal and less visual in learning preference may experience difficulty. Can a student who's a highly affective, relational learner succeed at a Research I institution, where most of the faculty she encounters in mathematics, science, and technical areas will teach in an analytical manner?
- Should the relationship of learning style research to educational outcomes affect what we do with faculty development?
- What new assessment methods are needed?
- Where's the next frontier to help us accurately evaluate and portray learning styles as they are impacted by diversity?

Once we've considered these kinds of questions, we can begin to think about reasons for not only doing more learning style assessment but also incorporating diversity. We may want to give students a learning styles–preference survey simply to give self-assessment feedback to students, so they can see themselves, maybe for the first time ever, as a learner.

We can go from there to doing cohort comparisons, looking at clusters of behaviors that we see in groups. For example: What clusters of behaviors are associated with success or failure in beginning science or math courses? What clusters of behaviors are associated with success or failure across what groups in engineering?

Next Steps

We are slowly moving from a generic model of learning style to a more comprehensive model that incorporates the diverse needs of all students and the unique needs of diverse groups, including their learning styles.

There is currently no effective assessment of learning styles and diversity that will enlighten us in significant ways about student performance, student success, student learning, etc. I'm working on an instrument that has been pilot-tested for reliability and validity at five institutions, and we will soon be pilot-testing it at five more. We're trying to develop an instrument that profiles generic learning styles and also correlates that information with other critical dimensions, such as student-student interaction and student-instructor interaction.

Given limited resources, what steps can institutions take to better address the needs of diverse learners? Begin by developing a strong teaching initiative around a more general area and then incorporate attention to diverse learning styles into it. At North Carolina State, a group called the Hewlett

Fellows focuses on inquiry-guided teaching and promoting active learning. Faculty are very enthused about it. But, if we had first tried to develop a learning style initiative focusing on effective teaching, I predict it wouldn't have been as successful.

Another possibility is to create cooperative clusters or learning communities, provided that they are designed to accommodate diverse groups. Diversity is not as present as it should be in learning community research. There's an inherent assumption that learning communities automatically account for diversity, but that's not true. For example, if you set up voluntary curricular learning communities, diverse students will not necessarily sign up. They do not see the inherent value of clustering across courses.

Cooperative clusters show promise, however. Sheila Tobias (1992, 1990) has studied cooperative clusters associated with the success of women in science and mathematics. Uri Triesman (1992) has done the same with underrepresented students and students of color, especially in mathematics.

But cooperative learning models don't attract everyone. A student who is introverted and less-skilled and doesn't understand the culture of college is not going to be assertive in cooperative learning approaches. That student will not participate actively in learning communities, and that student will be silent in chat rooms.

It's a challenge to address the needs of diverse learners, because it's so difficult to reallocate resources from things that aren't really significant and don't yield outcomes of consequence. But we should do faculty development on this subject, and we should have something for students coming into our institutions who historically have been identified as having the most problems. If we don't do that, why keep bringing them in? They'll just continue having problems. These are two areas in which we should all invest resources.

References

Tobias, S. (1992). *Revitalizing Undergraduate Science: Why Some Things Work and Most Don't.* Tucson, AZ: Research Corporation.

——— . (1990). *They're Not Dumb. They're Different: Stalking the Second Tier.* Tucson, AZ: Research Corporation.

Triesman, U. (1992). "Studying Students Studying Calculus: A Look at the Lives of Minority Mathematics Students in College." *College Mathematics Journal, 23* (5): 362-372.

Willis, M.G. (1989). "Learning Styles of African American Children: A Review of the Literature and Interventions." *Journal of Black Psychology, 16* (1): 54.

James Anderson is vice provost and dean of undergraduate affairs at North Carolina State University.

A Few Good Measures: The Impossible Dream?

by Victor M. H. Borden

Let me begin by noting that I'm an institutional researcher. As you may know, institutional researchers have all the answers, but we don't, unfortunately, have the questions. So I'm going to take you on a journey to figure out what the questions are, rather than what the answers are.

Since I've worked with Trudy Banta for eight years or so, I know that one always starts with a purpose. So that's where we'll begin: My major purpose is to help you determine whether it really is possible to have a few good measures. What will the answer be: yes or no? Well, it depends — on what you mean by "few," on what you mean by "good," and, as President Clinton enlightened us, on what you mean by "is."

And if by chance we figure out that there *aren't* a few good measures, then how, where, when, and in what context can performance measures be useful? My second purpose is to address this question.

My third purpose is to explore some organizing concepts that may be useful in developing performance measures. My final purpose is to help you realize that no one else has figured all

this out. Lately, when I attend conference sessions on performance indicators, I worry that someone else has it figured out. I have yet to have my worries confirmed.

What Is a Performance Indicator?

Performance indicators — or, as I'll use the term interchangeably, *performance measures* — mean many things to different people. At a recent site visit for an evaluation project in which I'm involved, Peter Ewell characterized performance measures as a way to tell someone something about what you do. Peter's simple characterization stuck in my mind. I'd like to add slightly to this simple definition: Good performance measures also tell something about how well you do it, whether it works, and what your plans are for improvement.

Most people also expect performance indicators will be quantitative, with a specific statistic, number, or perhaps a trend line that shows what and how you've been doing.

For many people, performance indicators are something that gets done *to* you rather than something *you* do, somewhat like taxes or a bad cold. But, because the best defense is a good offense, I'll focus my comments on how you can be involved in developing performance measures proactively, rather than reacting to external mandates.

And now, a song for inspiration (to the tune of "Just My Imagination"):

I look at my email, a message from way
  on high,
The chancellor wants measures that all
  our constituents will buy,
To please the board of trustees, state
  legislators of every sort,
That will also improve our ranking in
  U.S. News & World Report.
I whip out my palm top remote access to
  the PeopleSoft Data Mart,
Download value-added learning
  outcomes, and that was just a start.
Faculty workload, courses taught,
  grants obtained and awards,
The impact of our civic engagement on
  communities that we support.

But it was just my imagination running
  away with me,
It was just my imagination, running
  away with me.

Soon, there'll be measures, on which we
  can all agree,
All our constituents and stakeholders
  will clearly see,
The faculty do more than just work for
  themselves,
And institutional researchers write
  reports that don't just sit on shelves.

But it was just my imagination running
  away with me,
It was just my imagination, running
  away with me.

It All Depends on Your Perspective

Determining which performance indicators are best for your situation depends on three factors: the unit level in which you work (e.g., department, school, institution, system), your role in that unit (e.g., chair, dean, provost), and your target audience (e.g., your faculty, prospective students, the state legislature).

Let's think of some potential indicators, either from the audience perspective or from the provider perspective. Suppose, for example, that your unit is college- or university-wide, your role is provost, and your audience is your faculty. You want a few good measures for internal accountability to your faculty. What are some possibilities? The employment ratio of graduates, employer satisfaction with student performance, graduation rate by major, the number of people who take required courses at your institution as opposed to another college or another provider, licensure pass rates . . . all are candidates that might be appropriate.

Now suppose you are provost again. What would you want to tell prospective students? Perhaps the percentage of students going on to graduate school, student employment outcomes, student satisfaction, the quality of your programs, or information about technology and innovation.

Now let's move to the audience side. You're a student. What would you want the provost to tell you? Perhaps the average starting salary of recent graduates, opportunities for meaningful interaction with faculty, class size or the student/faculty ratio, the acceptance rate at professional schools, classroom resources, transferability of class work, and cost.

Now suppose you're a member of the faculty. What would you want the provost to tell you about how your college or university is doing? Perhaps faculty salary benchmarks, equity in allocating positions, quality of incoming students, or student satisfaction.

Now let's say you're a provost talking to a state legislator. What do you want her to know about your institution? Perhaps the graduation rate of first-generation students, retention rates, the number of students graduating in four years, cost per degree, percent of graduates remaining in the state, student competency, licensing pass rates, grant funding, the percentage of lower-division student credit hours taught by full-time tenured faculty, the number of registered voters in the legislator's district attending your college, hours of community service per student, and enrollment and retention rates of students of color.

As you can see from these examples, it's not difficult to come up with many good measures. Our original question, however, was whether it is possible to come up with just a few. To answer this, I will first take you through a somewhat personal tour of my experiences in developing performance indicators, and then consider some emerging trends.

Lessons Learned From Scholarship and Theory

Measurement theory posits that measures exist only within a context of ideas, concepts, or theories. Measures should address how those ideas are manifest in observable behaviors, objects, or events. From these empirical observations, we can then reassess and refine our concepts and theories. We know this as the "inductive-deductive cycle": conceptualizing, hypothesizing, measuring, and generalizing in a recurrent or perhaps spiraling cycle. Without this cycle, measurement has no meaning. Peter Ewell and Dennis Jones (1994) boil the inductive-deductive cycle to a few key words: "Above all, think before you count" (34).

In his book *Conceptualization and Measurement in the Social Sciences*, Blalock (1982) notes that "unless very careful attention is paid to one's *theoretical* assumptions and conceptual apparatus, no array of statistical techniques will suffice" (9). This is a fancy way of saying "garbage-in, garbage-out," which is demonstrated by many performance measures that we now use, including graduation rates and funding per FTE. Do these measures tell us anything meaningful? Are they measuring the same things across different places? Are they comparable? (We know the answer: Comparability is very limited.)

Trudy Banta and I co-edited a volume of New Directions for Institutional Research, entitled *Using Performance Indicators to Guide Strategic Decision Making* (Borden & Banta 1994). I will now share the sound bite lessons that I believe emerge from each of the chapters of that volume, one of which I've already mentioned. [Chapter authors are indicated parenthetically.]

- Where you stand on performance indicators depends on where you sit: your perspective and your role (Borden & Bottrill);
- Think before you count (Ewell & Jones);
- In Europe, performance indicators are "out"; quality assurance is "in" (Jongbloed & Westerheijden);

- PIs are useful, if the P stands for "process" (Dorris & Teeter);
- Key performance indicators can be the fuel for a strategic decision engine (Dolence & Norris); and
- Activity-based costing can yield performance measures relating to the costs of doing business (De-Hayes & Lovrinic).

I'll go into just a little more depth about one of these chapters to illustrate the kind of thinking that emerges if you go beyond the sound bite level of analysis, which is *not* common among many purveyors of performance indicators (especially the externally mandated kinds).

Although we usually think of performance indicators as measures of independent aspects of an institution's performance, Michael Dolence and Don Norris suggest in their chapter that it is important to consider the interaction of strategic initiatives across performance indicators. For example, average section size and cost per credit hour are two potential college or university performance indicators that are often inversely related: As section size decreases, costs typically increase and vice versa. Dolence and Norris propose an interesting and engaging group process for examining the impact of strategic initiatives across key performance indicators. As with all such planning processes, the greatest value is derived more from the process than from the product.

In the concluding chapter, Trudy Banta and I (1994) propose five criteria for effective performance indicators:
1. They start with purpose.
2. They are aligned throughout the organization.
3. They are aligned across inputs, processes, and outputs.
4. They coordinate a variety of methods.
5. They are used in decision making.

Lessons From the American Productivity and Quality Center

In another chapter of my life, I participated with representatives of about twenty other universities in an American Productivity and Quality Center (APQC) benchmarking study called "Measuring Institutional Performance Outcomes" (APQC 1998).

For the benefit of those of you who are not familiar with APQC benchmarking studies, they employ a largely qualitative method to identify institutions, both inside and outside of higher education, that are exemplars in the target activity of the study. Through a series of group project meetings and site visits to the "best practice" institutions, study participants identify a set of emergent themes that characterizes best practice.

The following themes emerged from the study in which I was involved:
- The best performance measures communicate the institution's core values.
- Good institutional performance measures are carefully chosen, reviewed frequently, and point to action to be taken on results.
- External requirements can be extremely useful as starting points for developing institutional performance measurement systems.
- Performance measures are best used as "problem detectors" to identify areas for management attention and further exploration.
- Clear linkages between performance measures and resource allo-

cation are critical, but the best linkages are indirect and non-punitive.

- Performance measures must be publicly available, visible, and consistent across the organization.
- Performance measures are best considered in the context of a wider transformation of organizational culture.
- Organizational cultures supportive of performance measures take time to develop, require considerable "socialization" of the organization's members, and are enhanced by stable leadership.
- Performance measures change the role of managers and the ways in which they manage.
- You cannot "lead" with performance measures.
- Performance measures emerge from a broader culture of evidence — that is, they are part of something bigger.

But the major conclusion of the APQC study, in my estimation, is that there is probably no single set of a few good measures, which answers our first question.

Having said this, I will admit that one of the non–higher education institutions identified as a best practice partner in the APQC study did have a single set of five performance measures. However, these five measures belie far more extensive information-based analyses, measures, and evaluation processes that are going on underneath the surface.

Lessons From the IUPUI Experience

During my eight-year tenure at Indiana University Purdue University Indianapolis, the university has undertaken three approaches to developing and using performance indicators.

I call the first one the "laundry list" approach. We started with the five major strategic themes described in our mission statement: student learning, responsibilities for excellence, centrality and community connections, collaboration, and accountability and best practices. Each of these themes was further elaborated by three to eight institutional goals, for a total of twenty-nine institutional goals.

The twenty-nine institutional goals were not exactly concretely measurable concepts. For example, one of the goals within the theme "Responsibilities for Excellence" was "Having expert faculty in all our disciplines whose teaching and scholarly work are respected and celebrated within and outside the institution." What measure might we use to assess whether we have attained this goal? Obvious possibilities include the number of rewards and recognition attained by our faculty, their presentations, publications, editorial board memberships, and so on.

I've just quickly rattled off four concrete measures for one of the twenty-nine institutional objectives specifically mentioned in our strategic plan. If that is an average number, then we are now up to about 120 indicators total.

Then consider the questions we would have to resolve in order to measure just one of these indicators: number of articles published in refereed journals. First, is that an adequate definition? Or do we need to consider the "quality" of each journal? Second, have you ever tried to collect reliable information from a faculty body numbering more than 1,500 on any aspect of faculty scholarship?

As you might imagine, this "laundry list" approach died of its own weight very quickly.

I call IUPUI's second approach the "performance report" approach. Under this approach each school prepares an annual report of its activities — what was done well, and what measures were used to make that determination. The central planning support staff review these documents in search of examples to include in an annual campus-wide summary of accomplishments relating to the institution's strategic themes, goals, and objectives. We (i.e., the central planning support staff) then develop some quantitative summaries that relate to the general theme areas (e.g., student learning), without worrying about covering every specific goal and objective. Finally, we include an appendix of other general quantitative trends related to students, faculty, staff, and budgets.

The first year we prepared this report, we noticed how our available measures were unbalanced relative to IUPUI's strategic themes. For example, we have a lot of data on student enrollment, but not as much on student learning or on centrality and community connections.

This approach nonetheless produces a report that is closely aligned with real institutional planning, reporting, and improvement efforts. If we improve our planning, reporting, and improvement efforts, the annual performance report should become better, perhaps even including something we might recognize as a set of performance measures.

As an outgrowth of this approach, we have begun to rethink our broad-stroke planning and evaluation processes, leading to IUPUI's third approach, which I call the "Core Mission–Core Indicators" approach. Realizing that the clarity and succinctness of our performance indicators are necessarily tied to the clarity and succinctness of our mission, we started by revising our mission statement to a much simpler statement:

The VISION of IUPUI is to be recognized as one of the best urban universities. For IUPUI, achieving the status of an outstanding urban university means demonstrating:
- *Effective Student Learning*
- *Excellent Research and Scholarship, and*
- *Exemplary Civic Engagement*

Our task now is to identify indicators within these three categories. Our early thinking suggests that we may be able to come up with far fewer indicators than the 120 or so inherent in our laundry list process.

Within the "Effective Student Learning" mission, we've identified two kinds of goals: enrollment management and student learning. Within enrollment management, we examine the quality and diversity of incoming students, rates of student progress, student satisfaction, and transfer articulation and success. Within student learning, we examine assessment results, licensure rates for professional programs, students' self-perceptions of learning gains, and employer ratings of skills and competencies. Assessment results aren't really a performance measure, because you can't boil them down to a single meaningful number, but you can use an indicator to demonstrate that you have them.

Within the "Excellent Research and Scholarship" mission, we look at grants and funding, awards and recognitions, National Centers of Excellence, and the ISI database, which provides information on citations of articles written by faculty.

Within the "Exemplary Civic Engagement" mission, we examine our contributions through education and research, specifically elements of the curriculum that use the city, retention of graduates in the area, research on urban topics and with urban partners, and economic impact. We are also looking at using a model developed by colleagues at IUPUI for assessing the scholarship of service (see *Service 1999*). The model looks at four aspects of civic engagement: (1) its impact, (2) the intellectual nature of the work (e.g., command of expertise, innovation, interdisciplinary nature), (3) the sustaining contribution (e.g., its developmental complexity, whether leadership serves as a catalyst), and (4) communication through multiple and diverse professional modes.

The Urban Universities Portfolio Project (UUPP)

Can a portfolio be a performance indicator? What if, instead of creating a quantitative measure, an institution distributes a portfolio of student work, teaching, and other institutional activities? Is that a performance indicator?

IUPUI has developed an institutional portfolio through its participation in the Urban Universities Portfolio Project.[1] In it, we provide indicators for our three major mission components: Effective Student Learning, Excellent Research and Scholarship, and Exemplary Civic Engagement. Within student learning, the portfolio answers basic questions such as who enrolls, what kind of programs support these students, and what evidence shows that the programs work.

The section on our learning communities and their impact on students, for example, includes a blurb of a study examining the impact of participation on student progress and performance. The portfolio gives access to the whole report to anyone interested.

An institutional portfolio can thus serve as a single campus indicator.

As part of the UUPP project, we are meta-analyzing the portfolios of the six participating institutions to see what we have in common as urban universities. Our working themes include access and support, diversity and pluralism, the urban context for student learning, the urban university as an intellectual resource, and civic engagement.

In another project in which I'm involved — UUSPP, for Urban University Statistical Portrait Project (not to be confused with UUPP) — my colleagues and I are using the six themes that emerged from the UUPP meta-analysis as a starting point for developing measures that represent the effectiveness of urban mission universities better than do current popular ones (e.g., retention and graduation rates).

I hope you've noticed the recurrent theme in these institution-specific and consortia-based efforts I've just described. In all these examples, most of our time and effort is devoted to defining and refining the broad themes (concepts) by which we think our performance should be measured. In my opinion, far too much time is wasted developing performance measures, without nearly enough thought given to what we are trying to measure.

Emerging Approaches

If you've been following the literature on performance indicators, you've probably read a lot lately about dashboard indicators and balanced scorecards. Personally, I don't like the term "dashboard indicators," because I'm not sure who's driving, where we're going, and whether we're viewing this from the front seat or the back seat. It's very much of a command-and-control orientation. It's not yet clear whether dashboard indicators can be used for improvement as well as for accountability.

Balanced scorecards, as the name suggests, present a more balanced approach. Rather than review balanced scorecards in detail here, I recommend that you read "Toward a Balanced Scorecard for Higher Education," by Brent Ruben (1999) of Rutgers University. Following Kaplan and Norton's (1992) original formulation, Ruben proposes that a balanced scorecard incorporate four perspectives: performance outcomes, constituency satisfaction, internal business process, and learning and innovation.

Ruben does a great job of spelling out the inadequacy of the "accounting-based" measures that have dominated performance indicators in higher education:

- They are too historical;
- They lack predictive power;
- They can reward the wrong behavior;
- They focus on inputs, not outputs;
- They may not capture key business changes until it's too late;
- They relate to functions rather than cross-functional processes;
- They give inadequate attention to difficult-to-quantify resources, such as intellectual capital.

We've been aware of these concerns for years, and he expresses them very well.

Ruben suggests that we should study the three basic areas that represent the core of most of our missions: teaching/learning, scholarship/research, and service. He also suggests two other internal areas of focus to round out the balance: workplace satisfaction and finances. As another example of his adaptation, Ruben describes two major themes for performance indicators of teaching/learning: the quality of products (courses and programs) and student outcomes. [2]

A Few Concluding Precepts

Returning to our original question: Is it possible to have a few good performance measures? A few good measures are, in fact, possible if you have a very focused mission and a very targeted clientele. The rest of us need more than a few good measures.

Refining the criteria Trudy Banta and I proposed in our 1994 monograph, I offer the following characteristics for effective performance indicators:

1. They should be designed using conceptually and methodologically sound procedures.
2. They must be mission-related, reflect core values, and aligned throughout your organization. In other words, they should reflect what your institution actually does in the way of planning and evaluation.
3. They should be developed for targeted audiences.

Consider involving important constituents (faculty, students, employers, research partners, etc.) in the next iteration of your mission statement and the indicators you will use to stimulate internal improvement and external accountability.

I think you will find that you need to come up with not just a few good measures but a broad range of measures that meet the needs of various constituent groups. You may end up with more than a few good measures, but you only need communicate them a few at a time.

Finally, what's the point of having performance indicators if they're not used for continuous improvement. You've got to close the loop. In the final analysis, performance measures are only worthwhile if they can be used to help your unit or institution attain its goals and objectives.

Notes

1. AAHE and IUPUI are partners in this Pew-funded project, "The Urban Universities Portfolio Project: Assuring Quality for Multiple Publics." The project engages six such universities in the creation of institutional portfolios and in an innovative auditing process. The participating campuses are California State University-Sacramento, Georgia State University, IUPUI, Portland State University, the University of Illinois-Chicago, and the University of Massachusetts Boston. For more, visit AAHE's website at <www.aahe.org>.

2. Since giving this presentation, I've combined some of Ruben's ideas into IUPUI's evolving performance indicator and institutional portfolio efforts. The latest model for IUPUI performance indicators is now portrayed in the "Performance Indicators" section of the IUPUI institutional portfolio at <http://www.imir.iupui.edu/iupuifolio>.

References

American Productivity and Quality Center. (1998). *Measuring Institutional Performance Outcomes.* Houston, TX: APQC.

Blalock, Jr., H.M. (1982). *Conceptualization and Measurement in the Social Sciences.* Beverly Hills: Sage.

Borden, V.M.H., & Banta, T.W. (Eds.). (1994). *Using Performance Indicators to Guide Strategic Decision Making.* New Directions for Institutional Research, No. 82. San Francisco: Jossey-Bass.

Includes the following chapters:

Banta, T.W., & Borden, V.M.H, "Performance Indicators for Accountability and Improvement," pp. 96-106.

Borden, V.M.H., & Bottril, K.V., "Performance Indicators: History, Definitions, and Methods," pp. 5-22.

DeHayes, D.W., & Lovrinic, J.G., "Activity-Based Costing Model for Assessing Economic Performance," pp. 81-94.

Dolence, M.G., & Norris, D.M., "Using Key Performance Indicators to Drive Strategic Decision Making," pp. 63-80.

Dooris, M.J., & Teeter, D.J., "Total Quality Management Perspective on Assessing Institutional Performance," pp. 51-62.

Ewell, P., & Jones, D., "Data, Indicators, and the National Center for Higher Education Management Systems," pp. 23-36.

Jongbloed, B.W.A., & Westerheijden, D.F., "Performance Indicators and Quality Assessment in European Higher Education," pp. 37-50.

Kaplan, R.S., & Norton, D.P. (1992, January-February). "The Balanced Scorecard — Measures That Drive Performance." *Harvard Business Review*.

Ruben, B.D. (1999). "Toward a Balanced Scorecard for Higher Education: Rethinking the College and University Excellence Indicators Framework." Baltimore, MD: The Hunter Group. Retrieved September 25, 2000, from <www.hunter-group.com>.

Service at Indiana University: Defining, Documenting, and Evaluating. (1999). Indianapolis, IN: Indiana University Purdue University Indianapolis, Center for Public Service and Leadership.

Victor Borden is associate vice chancellor for information management and institutional research and associate professor of psychology at Indiana University Purdue University Indianapolis.

Assessment of Innovative Efforts: Lessons From the Learning Community Movement

by Jean MacGregor, Vincent Tinto, and Jerri Holland Lindblad

The interest that's brought the three of us together has been that strand of innovative work known as learning communities, particularly the assessment of learning communities. Our remarks here will be framed, however, not only in the context of issues associated with learning community assessment but also as lessons for the assessment of any innovative work.

We will begin with a brief overview of curricular learning communities to give you a sense of the water in which we all swim. We will then report briefly on research on the state of learning community assessment. We will follow that with some ways to frame assessment efforts that are particularly ap-

propriate to innovative work. We will conclude with a few stories about learning community assessment and some lessons learned from them.

What Is a Learning Community?

The phrase "learning communities" is used in many contexts today, including individual classrooms as learning communities, learning communities in residence life programs, and more recently, virtual learning communities. We will use the term here to represent curricular approaches that link classes, often around interdisciplinary themes, and enroll common groups of students for a quarter, a semester, or in some cases even a year. We see such learning communities as a very intentional restructuring of time, space, and student life.

There are multiple purposes for learning communities, and that's why they're a powerful kind of venue. The fundamental aim of learning communities is to deepen learning, create a deeper sense of connection among ideas and curricular issues, and create a stronger sense of community. More specifically, learning communities aim to promote the higher level of student engagement and success that comes from deeper intellectual interaction. Many of these programs aim to foster the complex thinking skills that come from examining ideas in an interdisciplinary context. They also aim to foster a social as well as an intellectual community. Learning communities can be powerful for teachers as well: Teaching in a common enterprise with common students can increase faculty vitality and enhance repertoires of teaching practice.

Learning communities put courses that are usually enrolled in and taught separately into larger, more coherent programs of study. This is not a new idea. We can find examples of these kinds of linkages going back to the 1920s under a variety of names. In the last fifteen years, however, interest in expanding these kinds of programs has grown. In an interesting intersection, it's in those same fifteen years that assessment has emerged on our campuses and become a priority.

Because learning communities are developed at all kinds of institutions with all kinds of curricular configurations, it's almost impossible to create or present a typology that includes all learning communities. But we can visualize a generalized set of types on a con-

tinuum from simple to complex curricular linkages, from minimal faculty coordination of the curriculum to a fully coordinated, team-taught program.

In its simplest form, a learning community might be composed of a small group of students that travels together, without faculty coordination, to stand-alone classes that also enroll other students. The student group often also meets in an additional, integrated seminar to discuss concepts addressed across the classes. For example, the students might take courses in history, film, and American literature, and the seminar might explore the question "What is the American character?"

At the next step on the hierarchy, a learning community may be composed of a cohort of students that takes a program of two or perhaps three courses together. The courses are linked thematically or by content, and the faculty teaching the courses plan the program collaboratively. Developmental students might, for example, take an intermediate algebra course linked to a precollege chemistry course. At several institutions, this "CheMath" program is preparatory to entering and passing college chemistry. The algebra and chemistry teachers work together to build basic concepts in chemistry and integrate that with algebraic thinking.

An example from the top of the hierarchy would be a fully team-taught program of courses that is embedded in an integrated program of study. For example, "Ecological Systems of Puget Sound" would include coursework in terrestrial and marine ecology, history of the Northwest, and statistics and mathematical modeling.

These examples show that learning communities have enormous variability in structure and content and in their degree of curricular coordination and co-curricular connections. They also have enormous variability in their pedagogies. In any given learning community, you might see intensive writing and peer editing, cooperative or collaborative learning, the use of technology, service-learning, and many kinds of integrative assignments and projects.

As with many other innovative efforts, learning communities involve a simultaneous change in both curriculum and pedagogy and often very different expectations of student work. They're complex innovations and complex interventions. Just tweaking a course a bit does not create a learning community; both the curriculum and pedagogy must be rethought.

Lessons From Assessments of Learning Communities

Like many innovations that are ambitious and labor- and resource-intensive, learning communities often find themselves immediately in the spotlight of scrutiny and pressed to prove themselves very quickly. Program innovators are therefore not only inventing new curricula and exploring new pedagogies but also often taking on evaluation responsibility as well.

Our colleague Faith Gabelnick often refers to this as the "poet-critic tension" in innovation. We ask faculty to invent, experiment, improve, and tweak in a new exploratory space. At the same time, we ask them to be critics, very quickly evaluating their work to prove its efficacy. Almost all learning community programs developed over the past fifteen years have been bootstrap, grassroots endeavors that have bubbled up among inventive, pioneering folks

who are pressed simultaneously to justify, evaluate, and prove. It's been messy but exciting.

In a review of the Washington Center's compilation of seventy assessment studies of learning communities, we found some promising results:

- Learning community students generally fare better academically, socially, and personally than those in comparison groups. This is especially true for at-risk students, underrepresented students, and students who generally make Cs and Ds — very good news.
- Learning community students' learning goes deeper, is more integrated, and is more complex than that of students in comparison groups.
- Learning community faculty make significant gains in personal, social, and professional development.
- The integration of academic and social life gives both faculty and students a sense of community.
- Faculty and students both develop sensitivity to and respect for other points of view, other cultures, and other people.

Our review also reveals gaps in what we know. First, we know little about learning community impact on a number of cohorts, including commuters, transfers, alumni, and administrators. We also need more information on underrepresented students, on faculty and student transitions in and out of learning communities, and on what brings about intended and unintended results.

Second, more than half the studies examined the most-integrated type of learning community, generally called "coordinated studies." We need more research on the less-integrated types of learning communities, such as Freshman Interest Groups, linked courses, and course clusters.

Third, we need more carefully planned studies that portray the spectrum with what researchers call "disinterested subjectivity."

Fourth, researchers and evaluators need opportunities to learn or re-learn qualitative and quantitative techniques. They also need time. Such opportunities are especially important in this era of performance-based funding. Sustained, rigorous, qualitative and quantitative assessment will contribute meaningfully to the growth and viability of innovations such as the learning community movement.

Planning an Assessment of an Innovative Program: Asking the Right Questions

Let's now use what we have learned about assessing learning communities to consider how to think about the assessment of such innovations. Unfortunately, when you're planning a program, how you will assess it is often one of the very last questions you ask yourself. But it shouldn't be your first question, either; a range of other questions often dictate what you end up doing and so should be considered first.

The first question you must ask when planning an assessment of an innovative effort is what *mode* you are in. Are you using assessment to improve the learning community? Or are you proving the value of the learning community in order to validate and/or institutionalize it? Those two modes give rise to very different ways of thinking about assessment.

Second, what are the *goals* of the innovation? What are the specific aims that it intends to achieve? These will tell you what outcome measures to focus on.

Third, who are the *audiences* with whom you intend to share the data and with whom you must hold a conversation about the evidence? If, for example, your mode is to prove and validate the learning community, you need to ask yourself whose support and participation you hope to gain. Faculty? Administrators? The president? State and foundation agencies? Other students or potential students?

Fourth, what *data* do you want to collect, and what methods do you want to use to collect those data? If, for example, you intend to prove to potential students that the learning community is worth enrolling in, you would need qualitative information such as student quotes. If, however, you need to prove the learning community's value to an administrator who is concerned about student retention gains, you'll need some numbers.

Finally, what are the *strategies* you will use to share the data? You know the old saw: Data not used are data not worth collecting. You must plan now how the data will be shared, with which audiences, and in which mode, because that will determine how you assess the program. Only after you've answered these questions can you design the assessment of an innovative program.

Now here are three examples to highlight the different ways learning community advocates have learned to do assessments for varying purposes.

1. Seattle Central Community College. In 1985, Seattle Central

Community College began experimenting with team-taught, interdisciplinary coordinated study programs, and the immediate feedback was very positive. The faculty teaching in the programs were excited; a few key administrators were very supportive; students seemed stimulated and pleased. There was some impressive data about rates of course completion and re-enrollment.

So all went well, in some ways. But the faculty teaching in the program wanted to convince themselves and their colleagues of the real texture of the program. Was it just a feel-good experience, or was it something substantive, of real value to students in their lives and their learning?

The faculty were looking for something more than the standard end-of-course, fill-in-the-bubble evaluations, which seemed unable to capture the complexity of what the faculty felt was happening in the classroom. They were also looking for a simple way to obtain information on students' perceptions of their learning community experience without intruding on student or faculty time and without disrupting the learning community's curricular focus or ethos.

The strategy the faculty struck upon was self-reflection. They asked students to write formal essays reflecting on their learning, not so much evaluating the program or the faculty but rather reflecting on themselves as learners, describing their experience and identifying benefits and challenges. In a blind study, volunteer faculty readers (not teaching in learning communities at the time) analyzed the essays to discern patterns and themes.

The results were quite positive.

The readers found that students very much valued the learning community experience in just the ways that most learning community teachers hoped they would. There was a genuine resonance between teachers' goals for the learning community and students' identification of those goals.

The more important and lasting results, however, weren't anticipated, a true lesson in evaluating innovative work. Students, on their own, without any prompting, regularly mentioned the very general-education outcomes the college had already identified as central to a degree. And the essays led to intense discussions among faculty on the language students used to talk about their experience, discussions that led to additional changes and improvements in the learning community program.

So the self-reflection exercise gave students a valuable experience and gave faculty a unique window on that experience. Within a year, all learning community teams began to use student self-reflection essays systematically. These reflective writing assignments have become a permanent fixture in all learning community teaching at this college.

A very modest effort to prove the efficacy of the program unwittingly became an enriched form of learning community pedagogy. A small, inexpensive, grassroots assessment effort had a very high degree of payoff — many unexpected results.

2. Spokane Falls Community College. Spokane Falls Community College had a well-established, well-regarded ten-year-old learning community program with campus support. Then, a sudden, complete turnover of senior administrators, a restructuring, a new focus on outcomes assessment, and an upcoming accreditation brought forth the occasion to do a major year-long study — a highly qualitative one — to address these constituencies and needs.

A team of eight learning community faculty members from disciplines across the college was trained in qualitative methodology. Using small, mobile research teams, they interviewed students, faculty members, and administrators with a wide range of perceptions about learning communities. They administered questionnaires to learning community students and a control population in three types of classes over three consecutive quarters. They pored over student class journals. The institutional research office collected some quantitative data for them.

The results affirmed the quality of the program and its significant contributions to the college: Faculty and students highly valued the richness of community they experienced. Students lauded the connections on and off campus that their group work experiences encouraged. No matter what the level of student ability, both teachers and students alike highlighted the intellectual gains and depth of learning that all types of learning communities experienced.

The team also identified weaknesses and needs and made plans to address them: training in engaging students in seminar discussions, mentoring for newer faculty members, increasing the numbers of learning community offerings and assessments, providing more and better space for learning community programs, and deepening collegiality across the college

by creating other community-building learning occasions. As an added benefit, the research team itself experienced a research process that mirrors the inclusive, collaborative, and conversational style of the learning community classroom. The study's outcomes also re-educated everyone — students, faculty, and administrators — about an innovation that many had come to take for granted.

3. Creating Powerful Assessments Through Multiple Methods. Multiple methods make for a more powerful assessment, one that not only helps document and explain the impact of a program but also allows us to discover other goals, perhaps unintended, that might have more impact on the program than expected beforehand. So our third example is from a national study of several collaborative learning communities across the United States. We collected quantitative survey information from program students and a matched comparison sample, as well as qualitative evidence, including interviews, observations, focus groups, and ethnographic research.

We learned that quantitative evidence is often very important in demonstrating impact. Our survey instrument, a variant of Robert Pace's Student Experience Questionnaire (1984), measured the amount of activity that students and faculty invest in the learning community, in the comparison groups, in course work, and in library work. It also assessed faculty and student engagement in writing and their perceptions of gain. Across the board, students in learning communities invested significantly more "time on task." The engagement clearly activated their involvement.

We also measured student perceptions of the environment, classes, other students, faculty, administrators, campus climate, and their own involvement. Again, across the board, students in learning communities perceived the environment more positively, themselves as more involved, and even perceived administrators as nicer. (So if you're an administrator, try learning communities!)

We also examined pass rates in developmental courses and continuation or persistence. For each measure, there were significant differences favoring students in learning communities. This held true both for developmental education students and for other students.

While these quantitative data document the effects of learning communities, they don't tell us why these effects occur. This is where qualitative studies help; they indicate the underlying dynamics that help explain what's happening. For instance, our qualitative findings showed that students find support through the activities that emerge from the collaborative exercises of the learning community. One student said, "The learning community was like a raft running the rapids of my life." She had two children, two jobs, and no partner in the house. The support she found in a learning community was critical to her managing to continue.

Some other quotations from our qualitative studies document how engagement leads to involvement in learning: "The more I talk to other people about the class stuff, the homework, the tests, the more I'm actually learning." "[I'm learning more] not only about other people but also about the

subject, because my brain is getting more [and] because I'm getting more involved with other students in the class." These quotations help explain why social engagement leads to learning gains.

One student adds, "I'm getting more involved with the class, even after class." For many students, the class becomes a peer group whose activities emerge from and expand beyond the classroom. George Kuh has a wonderful expression: a "seamless learning environment." We found that learning communities and collaborative pedagogies create seamless learning environments, expanding from the classroom out.

In learning communities, students learn to interact with people of different races, sizes, colors, etc. As a result, not only do they learn more, they learn better. It isn't just spending more time with others — it's the value students place on this powerful, diverse environment of learning from others. This is what students value most about a learning community.

We didn't expect to uncover the findings demonstrated by these quotations. As this example demonstrates, multiple methods, and qualitative methods in particular, allow you to not only explain but discover things you may not have thought of beforehand.

Thoughts to Reflect On

Two of these stories are examples of internal assessment work that were grassroots in nature and had positive impacts within their colleges in terms of communicating results. They contrast with our third story, which stems from a major national research project using multiple methods to study a variety of institutions. All three stories make clear that the struggles to make an innovative program work and to prove that it works must happen side by side.

There are several important lessons from the information we've shared.

- If any kind of innovative work is to expand and become more robust, we need to get much more serious about building both the practice and the assessment of that work.
- If you're not clear on the goals of an assessment and the audiences to which that assessment will be directed, it's hard to do the assessment well. So your first task is to ask yourself why, with whom, and for what purpose you are assessing, and then proceed.
- Gathering data isn't as important as using it strategically and communicating it to both receptive and not-so-receptive audiences.
- Finally, assessment work is never done. We can't assume that once an innovation is in place, our work is complete and our innovation will continue to be fully understood. Senior administrators come and go, events occur, and change happens, so the need to re-educate and re-develop will re-emerge!

That means hard work, but that hard work brings forth the opportunity for us all to learn.

Reference

Pace, C.R. (1984). *Measuring the Quality of College Student Experiences*. Los Angeles, CA: University of California Los Angeles, Higher Education Research Institute.

*Jean MacGregor is co-director of the National Learning Communities Project at the Washington Center for Improving the Quality of Undergraduate Education, at the Evergreen State College. **Vincent Tinto** is chair of the Higher Education Program at Syracuse University. **Jerri Holland Lindblad** is professor of English at Frederick Community College.*

Accreditation —
Where Credit Is Due

by Barbara Wright

Think, for a moment, about what students do that you *least* like. Some of us hate when students ask, "Is this going to be on the test?" or "What do I have to do to get an A?" Some of us wish they would work harder and spend more time studying. Why do these things bother us so much? It's because they embody a superficial, instrumental kind of approach to what we, as educators, consider the very serious business of learning.

The sort of student we're talking about here is not, alas, aiming for the joy of discovery, nor for the exquisite moment when he or she finally gets a difficult concept. Instead, the student seems to model rational choice theory with painful directness: How can I get the highest grade for the least investment? As educators, we want higher learning to transform students' hearts and minds. We want students to find the experience transfixing and transforming. Students, however, want to pass the course and get on with the rest of their lives. They know they can't afford to rebel, so they give us compliance but not much more.

What's interesting is that we often

don't behave very differently from such students. When I do workshops on assessment, I often begin with a rather cynical but commonly held definition of assessment: Figure out what "they" want, find the quickest, least damaging way to respond, send off a report, and then forget it.

The "they" requiring assessment is most often an accreditation agency. (A good 80 percent of the participants in a workshop I recently conducted for newcomers to assessment indicated that they were there at least in part because of accreditation.) Institutional response to accreditors is often, "What do you want from us? What do we have to do to get an A or at least not to fail?"

The problem with this cynical definition, of course, is that it takes a superficial, compliance-oriented view of assessment as an activity that's required but has no meaning, no integrity, no connection to anything the institution values, such as deeper learning or institutional transformation.

I begin with this definition because I'm a great believer in the psychological value of getting problems out in the open. I also believe in the pedagogical value of contrast. It is useful to talk about what the misconceptions are and how *not* to approach assessment before we get down to the hard work of thinking about how to do it meaningfully and well. This enables our assessment to address our institution's core questions and lead to improvement rather than a mere report.

All of this reminds me of fractals, which I first encountered about five years ago in a book by Margaret J. Wheatley called *Leadership and the New Science* (Berrett-Koehler, 1992). Fractals are visual or physical phenomena that repeat a familiar pattern or design at ever smaller or larger levels of scale. They can be created through chemical reactions or through computer-generated repetition of mathematical formulae. But they're also everywhere in nature: in cloud formations, in heads and branches and florets of broccoli, in trees and respiratory systems, and rocky landscapes that repeat their geological formations infinitely in boulders, rocks, and particles of sand.

Fractals are a useful metaphor for understanding the workings of organizational culture and for understanding why changing that culture can be so difficult. Small, local deviations are up against the immense power of the overriding design of the fractal-like culture. Conversely, if we can change the fractal's — or the organization's — design, there are repercussions throughout the structure.

We often hear that the ultimate purpose of assessment, beyond improving student learning, beyond understanding how our programs work, is to change institutional culture. In accreditation circles and elsewhere we often hear about the need to develop a "cul-

ture of inquiry" or a "culture of evidence." More recently, we've heard about the need to become "learning organizations." (It's been humbling to realize that, ironically, our institutions of higher learning haven't been able to become learning organizations much more readily than banks or manufacturers or trucking companies have.)

My aim here is to reflect on the ways in which assessment and accreditation have intersected over the past fifteen years, how they've helped each other to deliver, and the powerful effect that accreditation has had on the assessment movement. I will talk about what assessment has done for accreditation, what accreditation has done for assessment, and how I see the synergy working. Finally, I will address what I see as some of the limitations or dangers of this relationship, and close with a vision of where this dance may take us.

The Intersection of Accreditation and Assessment

The early- to mid-1980s were a time of widespread dissatisfaction with higher education, with flashy, sensational developments like state mandates, public outcry about rising tuition costs, tales of things college graduates could not do, draconian state budget battles, and performance funding. The thinking of the times was encapsulated in reports originating from both inside and outside the academy: "A Nation at Risk," "Involvement In Learning," "Integrity in the College Curriculum," "Time for Results," and so on. The reports invariably criticized the state of baccalaureate education and called for reform.

Conspicuously absent from these reports was any discussion of the role accrediting agencies had played or could play in improving the quality of the undergraduate experience. Accreditors were stung. Apparently they had become the victim of their own invisibility and discretion, thanks to their policies of confidentiality that prevented them from going public with either success stories or problem institutions. To make matters worse, accreditors focused on surrogates of institutional effectiveness, namely resources and processes, under the assumption that these surrogates led to quality education. In the rough climate of the 1980s, this turned out to be a dangerous assumption.

The contemporary postsecondary assessment movement began in earnest in 1985 with some early state mandates and AAHE's first Assessment Conference. The number of attendees and sense of urgency in the air stunned conference organizers. Sensing that something important was afoot, AAHE founded the AAHE Assessment Forum in 1987 with funding from the Fund for Improvement of Postsecondary Education (FIPSE). AAHE began to organize annual conferences, provide a much needed literature on assessment, and serve as a clearinghouse for ideas and information about model institutions.

Also in 1987, the U.S. Department of Education established new criteria for the recognition of all accrediting bodies, calling for a focus on educational effectiveness. Regional as well as professional accreditors were now expected to consider information on educational effectiveness systematically, as part of the accreditation process, and to determine whether institutions or programs "document the educational achievement of their students." In this way, federal

policymakers drew accreditation more directly into the process of holding institutions accountable.

The accreditation community's response was far from perfunctory compliance. It seized the opportunity to redefine and revitalize itself and refocus its processes. In 1985 and 1986 — before the Department of Education's new criteria were established — the Southern Association of Colleges and Schools (SACS) became the first regional association to adopt a major new standard on institutional effectiveness. Shortly thereafter, the Western Association of Schools and Colleges (WASC) followed suit. In 1989, the North Central Association of Colleges and Schools (NCA) weighed in with a new policy requiring that all institutions assess student achievement as part of self-study.

These associations were followed closely by the Middle States Commission on Higher Education, the Northwest Association of Schools and Colleges, and finally the New England Association of Schools and Colleges (NEASC).

All the regionals followed up with countless workshops, regional conferences, presentations at AAHE Assessment Conferences, and detailed manuals designed to support the new push to assess.

Recent Developments in Accreditation

Even more has happened in a second wave of assessment-related accreditation activity from 1996 to the present. Following a flirtation with SPREs ("state postsecondary review entities"), the U.S. Department of Education ratcheted up the pressure in the 1998 Higher Education Act reauthorization.

In the list of areas for which accreditors must have standards in order to meet federal compliance obligations, *student academic achievement* moved from ninth place to first. In other words, the federal government has deemed that academic achievement has primary importance, and this must be reflected in accreditation processes.

The regionals have met this challenge by taking yet more radical steps. Some very interesting experiments are in progress. WASC, for example, has proposed a new framework for accreditation that is organized around two core commitments, institutional capacity and educational effectiveness, examined in a twelve-year review cycle.

The institutional capacity review, coming in the early years of the proposed cycle, will focus on some traditional inputs, such as institutional policies, structures, and resources, but will also ask how effectively these support teaching and learning. The goals are to develop more efficient models for presentation and evaluation of data, to keep data routinely updated and available (for example, on a website), and to significantly reduce the labor and dollars that institutions now invest in collecting capacity data for the traditional self-study.

The educational effectiveness review, a separate process, would occur at about the midpoint of the twelve-year cycle and focus on the institution's educational vision, its organization for learning, and evidence of effective student learning. The final six years of the cycle would be available for follow-ups as needed.

WASC's goals are to reduce the cost and cumbersomeness of the accreditation process but also to increase its usefulness to the institution by building what WASC calls "institutional capacity" and by facilitating educational improvement. All participants in the process would be supported with special training and best practices for reviewing data and determining educational effectiveness. WASC is now in the process of rewriting its handbook of accreditation so that its standards are streamlined and framed around these two core commitments. It's a fascinating model.

NCA has also undertaken initiatives that push the envelope of traditional accreditation practice. NCA recently conducted an exhaustive review of hundreds of self-studies in a systematic effort to identify institutions with successful assessment programs and to understand what sets them apart from institutions with either less-successful programs or none at all.

NCA has simultaneously launched its Academic Quality Improvement Project (AQIP), another reconceptualization of the accreditation process. AQIP's goal is to make accreditation a more potent force in educational reform by melding continuous quality improvement principles with accreditation.

Institutions that sign on with AQIP will be expected to participate in required workshops, carry out assessments and other activities, and develop processes for continuous improvement. Because strengthening student learning is the primary purpose of an educational institution, AQIP plans to develop a series of non-prescriptive questions to help institutions to conduct investigations into student learning:

"As long as an institution continues to participate in AQIP, working se-

riously to improve its processes and results, its accreditation will continue. For participating institutions, the formal reaffirmation of accreditation every seven years will be a simple validation process that should not require reports, team visits, or other costly or intrusive processes" [for more, see www.aqip.org].

While participating institutions are expected to make a considerable investment in AQIP activities, the payoffs are clear: The institution is clearly investing in itself, not in an accreditation process to satisfy an external entity; and the cost and intrusiveness of traditional accreditation are virtually eliminated. The AQIP and WASC initiatives share common goals. They both aim to make accreditation a more useful, less cumbersome, and less costly process for the institution, at a time when everyone, including accreditors, feels stretched to the limit by current workloads. The initiatives also thoroughly embed assessment in these new frameworks.

Other regional accreditors are engaged in equally serious, if less radical, endeavors. Middle States is rewriting its standards and at the same time revising its statement on characteristics of excellence. It is also engaged in an extensive and systematic effort to identify and train educators in the region who have an interest in assessment and educational effectiveness but no particular prior expertise in assessment or accreditation. These individuals are being trained both to serve as qualified visiting team members and also to bring their new expertise back to their home institution.

SACS has a reputation, with its notorious "the institution must" statements, of being the most onerously prescriptive of all the regionals. A close reading of SACS's guidelines reveals, however, that while institutions must do assessment, *how* they shall do it is not dictated. Examples or possibilities are merely suggested. Nevertheless, SACS is currently reviewing its standards, with the expectation that they will become less prescriptive. As with WASC and North Central, another goal is to make accreditation more efficient, less intrusive, more clearly driven by improvement, and less compliance-minded.

Taking a uniquely gentle incrementalist approach, NEASC surveyed its membership two years ago in order to better understand the state of assessment at New England colleges and identify their needs. The survey revealed considerable consternation and a strong desire to learn more.

During the following year NEASC sponsored ten training workshops attended by more than a thousand participants, which in turn led to many requests for campus workshops. In 1999-2000, NEASC convened a task force to develop an academic assessment protocol. NEASC's hope is that a straightforward, non-prescriptive set of improvement-oriented questions will help institutions implement appropriate assessment efforts and collect documentation in an institutional assessment portfolio.

Since 1992 the Northwest Association of Schools and Colleges has not had a particularly high profile in assessment. But commissioners reportedly take their assessment policy very seriously, to the point that some 70 percent of the region's focused interim reports are required solely because institutions have failed to show they are meeting expectations for assessment. Northwest's goals are to introduce more-flexible, less data driven, and more-qualitative approaches to assessment and to help institutions move from developing plans and collecting data to actually using data for change and improvement.

There are also notable examples of professional accreditation associations rethinking their requirements in light of the assessment movement. The Accreditation Board for Engineering and Technology (ABET), the National Council for Accreditation of Teacher Education (NCATE), and AACSB-The International Association for Management Education all spring to mind. As with the regionals, these specialized accreditation associations have shifted their focus from resources and other inputs to outcomes. Not only has this helped improve programs; it also has addressed criticisms from presidents that the focus by professional accreditors on resources was demanding too much of institutional budgets, to the detriment of liberal arts and non-accredited programs.

The Impact of Assessment on Accreditation

So what has assessment done for accreditation? The bottom line on the incredible amount of activity I've described is that, with prodding from the U.S. Department of Education and the savvy cooperation of accreditors, assessment has proven to be an extraordinarily useful tool. It has allowed accreditation to zero in on the crux of the matter — student learning and edu-

cational effectiveness. It has enabled accreditation to recast itself, give it new energy and purpose, make itself more effective, and increase its clout.

Today assessment has provided the cross-fertilization, the energy, for a second generation of accreditation reforms. Accreditation has never been more vital, more interesting, more service-oriented, or more useful to its member institutions than it is today. And it's still on a roll.

The Impact of Accreditation on Assessment

Turning the tables, what has accreditation done for assessment? Clearly, just as assessment revitalized accreditation, accreditation's insistence on assessment has kept the assessment movement alive and thriving. But accreditation has been a sleeper in this role, little noticed and something we hardly anticipated in the early years of the assessment movement.

Some pundits felt that the assessment movement was at halftime in 1990, with perhaps another five years left. Yet the flow of novices and the demand for training and information continue unabated. The assessment movement clearly outlived the prediction of a ten-year life span and, like accreditation, is still going strong.

To what can we attribute this longevity? Clearly one factor is that assessment has been a point of confluence for a whole series of new ideas and issues in education: new understandings of teaching and learning, critiques of traditional methods of testing and evaluation, new definitions of the disciplines, a search for durable knowledge in a time of epistemological instability, renewed concern about students' affective and values development, and on and on. It helps, too, that we have stunning examples of success, such as Alverno College and King's College.

I would argue, however, that the single most powerful contributor to assessment's staying power has been its championing by regional and professional accreditation.

To finance activities related to assessment and educational effectiveness, accreditation agencies have received sizable grants from sources including FIPSE, Davis, Knight, and the Pew Charitable Trusts. This flow of millions of dollars in funding has supported assessment as well as accreditation. It has enabled accreditation to contribute incalculably to the creation of human capital in assessment, not only through assessment materials and activities but also by motivating individuals to attend events such as AAHE's annual Assessment Conference.

Accreditation has also provided the external push that can be exploited by institutional leadership to get its own internal assessment effort rolling and to motivate individuals to get that necessary training. It has provided the perfect combination of requirement and freedom for the institution to define that requirement. In so doing, accreditation has reinforced assessment's own principles of good practice, emphasizing that assessment has to be in tune with the mission and core values of the institution, tailored to the local context, focused on student learning, and used for improvement, not mere compliance.

By changing its own emphasis, accreditation has shifted our conception of *quality* from one defined by reputation and resources to one defined by student learning outcomes and talent devel-

opment, or value-added. In so doing, accreditation, like assessment, is making educational quality more inclusive, more democratic, more egalitarian.

The Symbiosis Continues

The pressure from accreditors to focus on assessment has been slow but steady over these last ten or fifteen years. The rhythm of five-year reports and decennial reaccreditation may seem so sluggish as to be utterly ineffectual. But the rhythm has been inescapable, like the flow of a glacier. Watching a glacier move is about as exciting as watching grass grow, unless you're in the right place at the right time and an iceberg breaks off and crashes into the ocean. But glaciers do move, and they are powerful if not flashy. In their path they transport boulders, scour valleys, carve new riverbeds.

Likewise, while our attention is diverted by the babbling brooks of day-to-day policy shifts, yellow journalism about what students can't do now, or the latest rise in some college's already remarkable room, board, tuition, and fees, accreditation just trudges along. While administrators, legislators, or state boards may become distracted by other issues, accreditation keeps coming back, even if it does take five or ten years. Some schools have been asked two or three times now what they are doing about assessment and why it's taking them so long. They're beginning to get the message that assessment matters and it isn't going away.

One of the sources of faculty resistance, not just to assessment but to many initiatives, is the certainty of many faculty that they will still be on campus long after the current administrator and his or her initiative du jour have moved on. But now the immovableness of faculty has met its match in the low-key but irresistible force of accreditation.

You can see what has made the collaboration of assessment and accreditation so powerful. Accreditation and assessment haven't merely worked together on a discreet project. They have, instead, done something more complex and ambitious. They have begun to build a whole new infrastructure for teaching and learning, for improving it, and for being accountable for it. That takes time, decades. It progresses at a glacial pace, but eventually it transforms the whole landscape.

Some Cautions

Despite considerable success and a hopeful prognosis, accreditors do see distinct dangers on the horizon for their partnership with assessment. A major concern shared by virtually all the regionals is that assessment findings could be used inappropriately — tied, for example, to performance funding, or used punitively, all but wiping out the possibility for institutions to keep the focus on improvement.

Policymakers and politicians are in search of simple answers to difficult educational questions and do not always understand the uniqueness of individual campuses, the complexities of teaching and learning, the difficulty of assessment, and the madness of taking a single test score as a complete and correct indicator of institutional quality. The task facing all of us is to keep getting the message out that such actions are irresponsible.

Another concern is the possibility that assessment may become the new orthodoxy of accreditation, as formulaic

as counting the number of books in the library and the number of PhDs on the faculty and as capricious and anecdotal as old-style fact-finding interviews. Both assessment and accreditation need to guard against that, too.

New Challenges for Assessment and Accreditation

Assessment has challenged accreditation to grow beyond its traditional role. It has given accreditation a way to zero in on the tough questions of student learning and educational effectiveness. Accreditation has evolved, and now it is challenging assessment to ratchet up its intensity and creativity.

Accreditation has put serious money into assessment. What about campuses? Consciously or unconsciously, everyone follows the money, and campus folk have an exquisite sensitivity to what is really valued — and invested in and rewarded — as opposed to what receives eloquent lip service, period.

If assessment is going to mean anything at all, it has to be recognized as a legitimate contribution to scholarship and become a normal part of promotion and tenure considerations. Unfortunately, this is easier said than done. There appears to be an unwillingness to do this at the institutional level for both practical and more intangible reasons.

First, a change in scholarship focus could mean the possible loss of research grant funding and the dollars from indirect costs that grants bring in, dollars that research institutions in particular are very dependent upon. Second, there's the fear that a change in scholarship focus could lead to loss of intellectual prestige and hence attractiveness and with them competitive advantage, tuition, and development dollars. In other words, a decision to reward assessment may look to institutional leadership like unilateral disarmament.

Similarly, faculty may be unwilling to take a chance on the scholarship of teaching, learning, and assessment, even if there is institutional support for it, fearing the resultant inability to get another position elsewhere, since traditional research and publication is the coin of the realm. In other words, it's unilateral disarmament on the personal level. And this begins to sound like another fractal.

My point is that this is an opportunity for a new collaboration between assessment and accreditation. Working together from macro and micro levels, they can push together toward a multilateral acknowledgment that assessment is indeed important scholarly work.

In closing let me return to Margaret Wheatley and fractals. Like Wheatley, I believe fractals can teach us something interesting and important, not just about natural formations but also about human endeavors. For example, it's impossible ever to know the precise measurement of a fractal. Wheatley explains the simple, seminal fractal exercise that Benoit Mandelbrot, to whom we owe the concept of fractals, presented to colleagues and students. He asked, "How long is the coast of Britain?" As his colleagues soon understood, there is no final answer to this question. The closer you zoom in on the coastline, the more there is to measure.

Since there can be no definitive measurement, what is important in a fractal landscape is to note the quality of the system, its complexity and distin-guishing shapes, and how it differs from other fractals. If we ignore these qualitative factors and focus on quantitative measures, we will forever be frustrated by the incomplete and never-ending information we receive. What we can know and what is important to know is the shape of the whole, how it develops, changes, how it compares with other systems.

These words contain an extraordinarily important lesson for us, for the assessment movement, for accreditation, for all the institutions and organizations involved in postsecondary education. The cultural change that we seek cannot be achieved by mere measurement.

But if we step back from data gathering to interpret those data qualitatively, if we share our insights and work together to discern and define that new culture, if the communication and process of assessment that have proven so powerful on campuses can be carried out at higher levels of scale, then perhaps all of us together, from individuals or individual units or schools or colleges or campuses or associations or accreditors, will have a chance at transformation. We will have a new culture of assessment, one that focuses on the adventure of discovery, that is delighted by unexpected findings instead of terrified by them, that goes beyond data to develop narratives that capture the shape of what we've seen.

Discovery, and the telling of that story of discovery, should be joyous, playful, surprising, maybe even funny. "Wouldn't we all welcome more laughter in the halls of management?" Wheatley asks toward the end of her book. Wouldn't we all welcome more laughter in the halls of academe?

Imagine a world in which the fractal of drudgery and stress, of too much to do in too little time, is replaced at all levels — from students and faculty and librarians and administrators to the offices of accreditors — with the joy and laughter of discovery, of true, deep learning.

Utopian? Perhaps. I've been accused more than once of being a hopeless idealist. But at their best, it's this utopia on which assessment and accreditation are triangulating. Who wouldn't trade what is all too often bleakest higher education bureaucracy for a living, breathing, self-reflecting culture of teaching and learning?

Barbara Wright is associate professor of German at the University of Connecticut, a member of the board of the New England Association of Schools and Colleges, and a past director of the AAHE Assessment Forum.

Abstract of highlights of a plenary session at AAHE's 1999 Assessment Conference. Visuals that accompanied the full presentation may be viewed at <http://www.nchems.org/present-.htm>.

Assessment at the Millennium: Now What?

by Thomas A. Angelo, Peter T. Ewell, and Cecilia López

facilitated by Theodore J. Marchese

At least three sources motivate faculty and administrators to engage in the assessment of their students' learning. The first source is *accountability demands* from both accreditation agencies and state government. The second is changing conditions around us, specifically *growing diversification* in postsecondary education, both in delivery mechanisms and in the nature of our students. The third source is the shifting *paradigm of teaching and learning,* in which we are moving from a teaching-centered to a learning-centered approach and developing new pedagogies, curricula, and technologies to meet student needs better.

All three of these forces affect us all, no matter what our roles are, and they will impact assessment in many

ways in coming years. We will discuss how these forces are changing and the implications of those changes for assessment, and we will conclude with some thoughts on the major lessons of the assessment movement to date that can guide us as we move into the new millennium.

Accountability Demands

Accreditation activities have historically focused on institutional self-studies and evaluation visits by teams of peers. What we need to work on now are improvement-oriented alternatives to this model that focus on what students know and can do.

State governments are looking at performance measures and have already implemented some. As states become more sophisticated in identifying and using performance measures, their need will increase for comparable data sets across states.

As our assessment and accountability tools become more sophisticated, we may see more substantial consequences for failing to meet performance standards. The accountability paradigm will change to focus on institutional improvement, particularly on student learning.

Growing Diversification in Postsecondary Education

Most notions of academic accountability and assessment are based on the increasingly outdated paradigm that most students are of traditional college-going age, make their studies their exclusive full-time focus, and attend just one established college or university for the duration of their academic career.

This model fails to take into account the increasing diversity of our student body. The "traditional" college student has virtually vanished. Today nearly all students are non-traditional in one way or another; most work and attend college simultaneously. Our students are prepared in many ways, at many levels, and our programs and assessment methodologies need to address that.

This outdated model also fails to consider what we call the enrollment "swirl": the increasing tendency of students to attend more than one institution. Cliff Adelman's (1999) study of attendance and degree attainment found that 58 percent of baccalaureate recipients attended more than one institution and 22 percent attended more than two. This trend raises questions about quality control and attribution of product.

The implication for assessment is that we must develop instruments that can assess the contributions of each institution toward the eventual degree.

Finally, this old model fails to acknowledge the many new providers of postsecondary education, including for-profit institutions and corporate providers, and that the line between traditional and non-traditional providers is blurring.

The Teaching/Learning Paradigm

The notion of a shift from a teaching-centered to a learning-centered approach to higher education was introduced by Barr and Tagg in 1995. As with many educational movements, this shift is happening slowly, but the pace could pick up over the next few years.

The new teaching/learning paradigm is "customer-centered" — i.e., students, employers, and other key constituents have a greater role in deciding what's important to learn. Over the coming years, employers will continue to "up the ante" in their demands for employees with necessary skills.

The new teaching/learning paradigm includes a move away from knowledge-based learning outcomes that focus on facts and principles to "deep learning" outcomes such as the ability to apply knowledge and critical thinking and other skills. Deep learning should be important to us all, because employers, legislators, other key constituents, and the students themselves all want us to develop students' skills and abilities; it's what makes a college education worth the investment. But even more important is that today's world presents incredible challenges that can't be met by people who have superficial educations. The task before us is to be able to assess the complexities of deep learning.

Implications of These Trends for Assessment

All three of these major trends — accountability, diversification, and the teaching/learning paradigm — have implications for the theory and practice of assessment:

Increased demands for accountability mean that we need to better communicate the results of assessment to our constituents, especially those right on our own campuses.

Accrediting bodies need to find more effective ways to engage campuses. They need to shift the focus from assessment as an external mandate to assessment as a transformational tool and demonstrate the value of assessment to an institution and its faculty.

States, meanwhile, need to focus on what really matters: student learning. They will become more interested in linking assessment results to resources and accountability.

The increasing diversification of higher education implies that students, rather than institutions and programs, will become the primary objects of assessment, as they move through multiple higher education venues. Traditional academic credentials — grades and credit hours — are becoming less relevant and credible.

Both employers and consumers are increasingly demanding "degrees with integrity" (i.e., with certifiable skills), and assessment will probably move in the direction of providing such certification. We need to create certifications of student core competencies, especially those developed over a series of courses, in ways that have meaning and credi-

bility to employers. Authentic performance assessments, credible across higher education sectors, will likely predominate over standardized tests as we become more sophisticated at developing them.

The new teaching/learning paradigm also means that we must use assessment to help faculty and students optimize the teaching/learning process. We need more focus on the scholarship of teaching and learning. What kinds of technologies, for example, best promote what kinds of learning, under what circumstances, and for what students? Under what circumstances do students need to work together in order to maximize learning? When do students need not come together at all? When is a lecture hall setting the most effective?

We also need to use our evolving knowledge of assessment, teaching, and learning to raise our expectations of both faculty and students. Faculty need to learn how to do their own assessments rather than use externally imposed tools. Students, meanwhile, won't give us good assessment information until they not only understand how to complete assessments but also appreciate their value.

Because "add-on" assessments can be so time-consuming, it is increasingly important that we embed assessments in our usual teaching/learning activities. Assessments can be incorporated into capstone experiences, final exams, internships, and other learning activities that demonstrate development of key skills and understanding.

What Have We Learned?

We would like to conclude with some thoughts on what we've learned in the fifteen years that higher education has been focusing on assessment.

1. Start with what you already have. Most institutions don't realize the extent of assessment information already available. Begin your assessment effort, therefore, by rounding up assessment information you already have. Include "proto-assessments": information from internships, field experiences, and capstone classes in which students synthesize their learning and apply it to new situations.

Look at information that's available but not well captured, such as faculty comments on papers. What do those comments tell you about patterns of student strengths and weaknesses? Find points in the student's academic program at which you already collect some information; could you use that opportunity to collect something more sophisticated?

"Starting with what you already have" includes starting with what others have done. Take the time to find models in other programs and on other campuses, so you're not continually reinventing the wheel.

2. Build on success. Assessment requires an atmosphere of trust and goodwill. In reality, however, assessments are often generated by issues or crises — hardly trust-building circumstances. Use assessment to look first at successes and then build a shared language, trust, and goals. Find just one example of an assessment success on your campus. How and why does the program or pedagogy work so well? What lessons can be extracted and shared to build more successes?

3. Focus assessment on what matters most. What is most important at your institution? This should be stated in your mission, and it probably includes improving student learning; but verify this by looking at where your institution spends its money. Usually what is most important to us is what we're willing to spend time, energy, and resources on.

4. Everyone needs to know what's in it for them. Faculty and students need a common understanding of what assessment is and why it's important. The support of the president, provost, deans, and board is critical; without their active and enthusiastic support, assessment will not happen.

5. Treat assessment as a "core competence." If your institution is going to be competitive, address the needs of diverse students, and use technology effectively, it must do assessment and do it really well. Faculty can be convinced of this if they understand that assessment is nothing more than a scholarly activity turned on themselves. What's different is that it's a collective, not individual, responsibility.

6. Assessment requires a culture shift. Assessment isn't a once-and-done project and doesn't provide definitive answers. It is, instead, a continuous cycle of raising questions and finding some answers that raise more questions.

Assessment also requires a different leadership style. If assessment is to be effective, the findings must be used to make decisions about programmatic directions, resource allocations, etc. We can't do things in the same old way.

We're in a new millennium with new paradigms and new approaches — exciting ones that have great potential to lead us to greater excellence.

References

Adelman, C. (1999). *Answers in the Tool Box: Academic Intensity, Attendance Patterns, and Bachelor's Degree Attainment.* Washington, DC: U.S. Department of Education, Office of Educational Research and Improvement.

Barr, R.B., & Tagg, J. (1995). "From Teaching to Learning: A New Paradigm for Undergraduate Education." *Change, 27* (6): 12-25.

Thomas A. Angelo is associate professor and founding director of The Assessment Center, School for New Learning, at DePaul University. Peter T. Ewell is senior associate at the National Center for Higher Education Management Systems (NCHEMS) and a member of the AAHE Board of Directors. Cecilia López is associate director of the North Central Association of Colleges and Schools. Theodore J. Marchese is managing director of Academic Search Consultation Service and an AAHE Senior Fellow. At the time of this presentation, he was a vice president of AAHE and executive editor of Change *magazine.*

Abstract of highlights of a plenary session at AAHE's 1999 Assessment Conference.

Assessing for Quality in Learning

by John Biggs

A psychology undergraduate once said, "Memorize the important points, and you'll do all right on the test." Another student once said, "I prefer multiple-choice questions; they're just a matter of learning facts, and no analysis or critique required, which I find tedious. I also dislike writing and prefer to have a set of questions in front of me."

Both these students were short-changing themselves cognitively. They were using a "surface" approach to learning, getting by with minimal effort and using inappropriate learning methods, such as memorization, to demonstrate mastery.

As educators, we're looking not for such superficial outcomes but for performance-type outcomes: learning that brings knowledge to life. We want to encourage our students to move from surface to "deep" approaches to learning. Deep learning means using the high-level, abstract cognitive processes that we want our students to develop. It includes explaining, arguing, reflecting, applying knowledge to problems that aren't in the textbook, relating new problems to established principles, and

hypothesizing. Students who take a deep approach are fully engaged in learning.

We want to see how far students can move into this level of understanding, so our challenge is to design teaching/learning and assessment activities that engage our students in deep learning.

The Chinese Paradox

Our challenge as teachers is to provide teaching/learning activities that support deep learning, and to eliminate those activities that support only surface learning, such as an insistence on coverage. Consider a study of Hong Kong students in which I was involved. According to the theories my colleagues and I had developed, educators there seemed to be doing everything wrong. Classes were large, the atmosphere authoritarian, and the assessment system was run by an examination authority separate from the curriculum department. Students were taught not in their native tongue but in English.

We would have predicted that these students would be high in surface learning but low in deep learning. What we found was a paradox: Students from this culture were outperforming Western students. The reason was our Western insistence on coverage, which is the enemy of understanding. To go deep takes time. The Chinese mathematics curriculum is deep, while the American curriculum has been described as "a mile wide and an inch deep."

The Role of Learning Activities

How can we help students engage in deep learning? I use a remark by Tom Shuell (1986) as a "meta-theory" — overall framework — for my work:

If students are to learn desired outcomes in a reasonably effective manner, then the teacher's fundamental task is to get students to engage in learning activities that are likely to result in their achieving those outcomes. . . . What the student does is more important in determining what's learned than what the teacher does.

Determining our objectives and ensuring that they focus on deep learning skills isn't difficult. What's challenging is operationalizing those objectives to create teaching and learning activities that are true to the content and reasonably effective. Talking to students is the most common method we use to engage students, but it probably isn't the most effective.

One possibility is to use problem-based learning techniques. Under this model, our objective is that students will be able to solve problems. Our teaching strategy is giving them problems to be solved. They will need information in order to solve the problems, so they learn content as well as problem-solving strategies. How effectively they solve the problem is our assessment.

Aligning Objectives, Teaching, and Assessment

Providing appropriate learning activities isn't sufficient to engage students in deep learning. We know that students react differently to different assessment formats. When students study for multiple-choice tests, they most often describe themselves as memorizing. When they complete other assignments, they more often describe themselves as reading in depth and applying what they've learned. When students of teacher education used portfolios to apply psychology to teaching and reflect on their learning, they commented, "A portfolio is not merely an assignment to be handed in but a powerful learning tool for the student" and "My portfolio led me to think about many questions that I never think of."

Teachers have an ordered view of the educational process. First come our objectives: knowing what we're going to teach. We then design our teaching to match our objectives, and finally we design our assessments to match what we've taught.

Students, on the other hand, view this backwards. They see the assessment first, then learn accordingly, then at last see the outcomes we are trying to impart. This "backwash" approach is fine *if our assessments correspond to what we truly want our students to know.* If we ensure that our objectives are buried in our assessment, our students will learn what we want them to learn. We need assessment tasks that address the sorts of deep learning skills that we want to see.

Quantitative and Qualitative Approaches to Assessment

I've mentioned that learning objectives are central to successful assessment; if we get them right, the rest should plug in and follow. If this is so simple, why doesn't it happen?

A major reason is our quantitative approach to assessment. We reduce student performance to a measurement scale. We assume that knowledge comes in units, each either correct or incorrect, all worth the same amount. We further assume that it doesn't matter which units you get right, as long as you get at least a certain percentage of them right. We also assume that the percentage index works across students and across subjects. These are all inappropriate assumptions.

Another assumption we make when we use measurement scales is that the characteristic being measured is stable. This leads us to focus more on test-retest reliability and items that discriminate than on whether the tests relate to the curriculum.

To make matters worse, some institutions and jurisdictions have expectations, if not requirements, that each faculty member will award a limited number of As and Bs. If a certain professor awards As to 60 percent of her class, instead of congratulating her we hear groans about slack standards.

A final assumption about the measurement-oriented approach to assessment is that testing should be under standard conditions. Students learn under different conditions, however. Portfolios aren't standardized but can do an excellent job showing what students have learned.

For all these reasons, we need to move from a quantitative, measurement-oriented model to a qualitative, standards-oriented model. A standards-oriented model assumes that learning is cumulative but that it changes in structure as it grows and as things relate to one another in more complex ways. Under this model, learning should be assessed in terms of where students are in the evolution of that structure, and the final grade should represent that.

This model requires teachers to articulate the highest level of understanding that can be reasonably expected of students and how students should demonstrate that level of understanding. Teachers can do this, but often they aren't used to thinking this way. One approach is to pull together data on the comments teachers make on student papers and agree on what each type of comment says about the level of understanding demonstrated in the student's work.

Levels of Understanding

The key to creating assessments that promote deep learning is to have a clear framework for operationalizing desired levels of understanding. I use a hierarchical model, the "SOLO Taxonomy," that describes the growth of understanding (Biggs & Collis 1982).

At the *pre-structural* level, the student has seized on an irrelevant feature of the task. This occurs early on in learning, where the student misses the point of the lesson.

Then at the *uni-structural* level, the student picks up one relevant aspect, such as identifying a correct feature or carrying out a simple procedure.

As the student continues to learn,

he or she gradually acquires more and more aspects, but does not connect them. The student can now enumerate, describe, list, combine, do algorithms, and perform serial skills. This describes the *multi-structural* level of learning; the student has collected a set of bricks, but there is no blueprint for the building.

At the next level, the aspects are integrated, such that the student can show how everything comes together. The case is made and the phenomenon explained. The student can compare and contrast, analyze, explain causes, justify, relate, and apply. This is operating at the *relational* level; the bricks become a building. The major outcomes of any program should be at least at the relational level. Not all our teaching need be relational, but we should teach our students strategies that help them develop relational skills, and our assessments should match the level of understanding we want.

The final level of learning is the *extended abstract* level of understanding. At this level, students can go beyond what's been given them into abstractions in far domains. They can theorize, generalize, hypothesize, and

reflect. With their mastery of their discipline, they can question what is given and theorize about alternatives. This is what we want professionals in any discipline to be able to do. We want doctors, for example, to be able to use what they've learned to treat diseases and disorders that they've never seen before. By the end of an academic program, therefore, our grading should include assessment tasks that involve some extended abstract thinking.

The SOLO framework can be used to ensure that objectives and assessment tasks are aligned.

Conclusion

In order to assess for quality in learning, we must make our objectives clear in terms of what students are to learn, and then build learning activities and assessment tasks that develop and promote those skills.

Can we use a qualitative standards-based system? I believe so, and have described in detail how the alignment model can be used for designing university and college teaching in my latest book (Biggs 1999).

References

Biggs, J.B. (1999). *Teaching for Quality Learning at University*. Buckingham, UK: Open University Press.

———, & Collis, K.F. (1982). *Evaluating the Quality of Learning*. London: Academic Press.

Shuell, T.J. (1986). "Cognitive Conceptions of Learning." *Review of Educational Research*, *56*: 411-436.

An honorary visiting professor at the University of New South Wales (Australia) at the time of the 1999 AAHE Assessment Conference, **John Biggs** *is now honorary professor in the Department of Psychology at the University of Hong Kong.*

Executive Summary of a plenary session at AAHE's 1999 Assessment Conference.

Testing Disadvantaged Students: The Elusive Search for What Is Fair

by Sharon Robinson

Fairness is an important but elusive value in testing. I will describe several definitions of fairness in the context of testing and discuss their usefulness to us as we strive to improve testing products and how those products are used. I will conclude by suggesting a reasonable definition of fairness that we can all use.

It's important to begin by noting that *all* information we use to make decisions about students should reach a standard of fairness, including grades, letters of recommendation, and the essays submitted with college applications that may have been prepared with the guidance of a professional counselor. None of these, by itself, offers a completely fair consideration of what every student knows.

What Is a Good Test?

Good tests involve fairness from their very beginnings, in their design, construction, and administration. Good tests reflect the diversity of voices of all test takers. They undergo a rigorous review in which the questions are judged to be fair. Good tests have standard administration procedures, so the scores reflect students' unassisted performance. Scoring is as objective as possible. If scoring must be subjective, it is not influenced by student background. Finally, good tests have evidence of reliability and validity. We should require nothing less.

Defining Fairness as a Lack of Group Differences

In the first definition of fairness that I present to you, differences across groups are taken to be proof of test bias. It's not possible to defend this definition rationally; if this definition is correct, tape measures, scales, and other objective measures are "biased" because they show differences among groups. Group differences alone are not proof of test bias, because a test may reveal persistent, real, and important differences.

We know, for example, that the most effective way that high school students can improve their SAT scores is to take rigorous academic courses during their high school careers. The effect of such a curriculum outperforms all other strategies to improve test scores. But what about students who don't have access to a sufficient number of rigorous high school courses? We want to eliminate group differences, but the only way to do that is by improving access to the knowledge and skills that the test measures.

Defining Fairness by How the Questions Look

Another way to define fairness is by looking at how the questions manifest themselves. Some questions may include material that is not required by the purpose of the test but that some people find upsetting or provocative. For example:

- A question on an American history test that mentions "pioneers and their wives" would be offensive, because it implies that the wives were not pioneers.
- A reading passage that mentions "people from Spain who established the first settlement in Mexico" would be offensive, because it disregards the indigenous people already there.
- A question on the SAT on abortion would be unduly provocative, although on a medical exam it might be necessary.
- A question about slavery or con-

centration camps might be provocative, unless the test is about history.

Questions that exclude groups who would not have experience with the material (for example, questions on tax-free bonds or the game of polo) are inappropriate, unless the material is essential to what is being tested. Also inappropriate are questions that are intimidating or off-putting to some groups or that require regional knowledge. Students in Vermont may think of a muffler, for example, as something to wear, but students in New Mexico may think of it only as a component of a car. Tests are not bags of tricks; they are, rather, opportunities for students to show what they know.

In reality, there is little connection between judgements about how fair test questions appear to be and how the test actually performs with various groups. It is nonetheless important to eliminate even the appearance of unfairness.

Defining Fairness by Differences in Selection

This third definition is an opportunity to illustrate the incredible complexities we deal with when we discuss fairness. It also shows how definitions of fairness can contradict one other.

Many tests are used to predict future performance. The SAT, for example, is used to predict freshman grade point average (GPA). Higher scores tend to predict higher grades, and lower scores tend to predict lower grades. We use a statistical tool called *regression analysis* to make this prediction. If a particular group achieves lower grades than the regression analysis predicts, the test *over-predicts* those students' performance and unfairly advantages that group. Similarly, if a particular group achieves higher grades than the regression analysis predicts, the test *under-predicts* those students' performance and unfairly disadvantages that group.

I will use two common models of fairness to illustrate the difficulties in determining whether or not a test is fair. Under one model of fairness, a test is fair if it neither under-predicts nor over-predicts the performance of any relevant group. It is fair to individuals because their membership in a group is not a consideration in predicting their future performance. This definition doesn't help us, however, to increase the representation of underrepresented groups.

Another model of fairness suggests that we should add points to the scores of students in disadvantaged groups. Such models of fairness purposefully over-predict the scores of students in underrepresented groups to achieve some desired level of group equity.

In a psychometric sense, whether or not a test used for selection is fair depends on the model of fairness that is used. A test that is fair according to one of the models of fairness will be unfair according to the other model.

Defining Fairness Through Validity

Validity is the extent to which a test meets its intended purpose and inferences and decisions based on it are appropriate and backed by evidence. Under this definition, a question is fair if group differences are caused by valid aspects of the question. A test question is unfair, however, if it measures an aspect of the candidate unrelated to the purpose of the test.

For example, a mathematics question that contains difficult reading material may be unfair to people who have difficulty reading, because the purpose of the question is to measure math knowledge rather than reading ability. Reading material of the same level of difficulty may be perfectly fair if the purpose of the question is to measure reading ability. Because validity depends on purpose, in order to judge fairness under this definition, it is essential that we know what we want to find out from the test and then judge its validity in relation to that purpose.

How Should We Judge Whether a Test Is Fair?

You can see that the same test may be judged fair or unfair depending on which definition we apply. What steps can we take to ensure that the tests we are using are truly fair?

- Become an aggressive and informed consumer. Test publishers should be prepared to talk about the steps they have taken to ensure fairness, and they should provide documentation of their efforts.
- If the test itself is disclosed, look at its questions yourself. Do they seem fair? Ask the test publishers how they checked for fairness. How does each question perform among and between different groups?
- Understand the purpose of the test. If it is used for professional licensing or certification, is there a connection between the content of the test and what the job requires? If it is used for graduation, is there a connection between the content of the test and what was being taught? If there is a "cut" or pass-

ing score, how was it set? Some users set sliding "cut" scores based on supply and demand; that's invalid.

- Does the administration procedure make the test accessible under standard conditions to all?

There are no easy answers about validity and no perfectly valid test. People will disagree about how much validity evidence suffices.

So what is the best definition of a "fair" test? While it's important to check all sources of information for fairness, the best definition of fairness is validity. Ask yourself, "Will information from this test allow me to make a better-informed decision about this person? Are differences among scores based on important differences that inform my decision?"

Those who find access to a quality education elusive for some groups can help them find a chance of achieving it — and thereby performing optimally on tests — by following the three Ts:

1. *Tell* what is going to be taught. Involve diverse voices that contribute to defining the knowledge we value.

2. *Teach* what we will be testing. Give every student an opportunity to learn what we value.

3. *Test* the material that we teach; make sure that is what we test.

When we take these three steps, we will finally break the cycle of elusiveness of fairness in the way we test.

I welcome you to this call.

Sharon Robinson is senior vice president and chief operating officer of Educational Testing Service.